Jesus of Galilee

Jesus of Galilee

His Story in Everyday Language

Louis Baldwin

Judson Press ® Valley Forge

JESUS OF GALILEE

Copyright © 1979
Judson Press, Valley Forge, PA 19481

Library of Congress Cataloging in Publication Date

Baldwin, Louis.
  Jesus of Galilee.

  Bibliography: p. 137.
  Includes index.
  1. Jesus Christ—Biography.   2. Christian biography—
Palestine. I. Title.
BT301.2.B22   232.9'01   79–11587
ISBN 0–8170–0841–1

To Ginnie, with love.

Foreword

During the first half-century A.D., countless thousands of convicted criminals died in public shame on wooden crosses. Today they have faded into a nameless multitude, lost in the mists of history.

But one of them shines through those mists like the sun. Something evidently happened after his death on the cross, something that burnt itself on the minds of his comrades and drove them to overturn the Western World. The Establishment tried to eradicate them, just as it had tried to exterminate him. But their followers continued to circulate the message he had given, and within a few generations *they* were the Establishment—unfortunately for his message.

He was a person of moods and paradoxes: witty and serious, playful and wrathful, kind and intolerant, considerate and sardonic, practical and mystical, uncertain and decisive, circumspect and courageous. His story, especially the story of his battle with the ancient Establishment, has never lost its universal relevance to the human predicament. It has been told many times, from many different viewpoints. Yet it is so remarkable that perhaps one more time can never be too often.

This is essentially a harmony of the gospels in a modern idiom. It is not a new direct translation but is based on existing translations, interpretations, biographies, and Christologies. It is presented in the hope of offering a readable account of Jesus' public life, his fatal encounter with the authorities of his time and place, and the aspects of his character and personality that made that encounter inevitable.

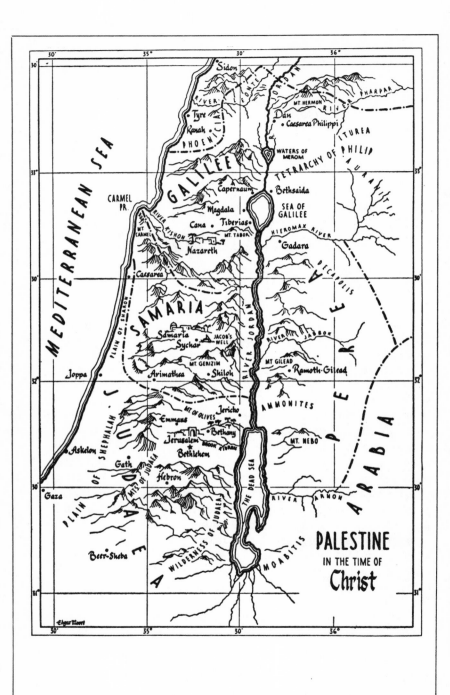

PALESTINE
IN THE TIME OF
Christ

Contents

Chapters

1 Prelude 11
2 First Skirmishes 17
3 Fall of an Ally 35
4 Forebodings 53
5 Threat and Defiance 65
6 To the Lions' Den 81
7 Defeat 97
8 Victory 125

Correlation with Gospel Passages 133
Sources 137
Index 141

Prelude 1

Great Expectations

For centuries various Hebrew prophets had foretold the coming of a Messiah. But the expected Messiah, as we might put it today, had an image problem: he (or, less probably, she) could be a military hero or a royal prince who could save the people of the one true God from the infidels, or he could be the "suffering servant" who could save them from themselves, as foretold by the prophet Isaiah.

For the Israelites had become more interested in calling themselves the people of God than in behaving like the people of God. As the "sons of Abraham," they had come to think of God as their particular property, to the exclusion of the rest of humanity. Prophets had arisen among them, warning them against such arrogance but almost never seriously denting their self-esteem. Their religious authorities nurtured that self-esteem with a mind-boggling collection of fussy rules and rituals, especially in the southern part of Palestine, in the province of Judea centered on Jerusalem. Love of God and neighbor was crowded out by anxious observance of inconsequentials. For example, since God had forbidden any work on the Sabbath, one had to be careful not to eat an egg that might have been laid on the Sabbath by an unscrupulous hen. It was small wonder that the people of Judea always seemed to be at least a little bit on edge.

Then into this china shop strode a rough fellow by the name of John, called "the Baptist" because he baptized people with water as a sign of their repentance washing away their sins. He lived and preached along the Jordan River and in the desert away from the towns; yet from Jerusalem and from all about Judea people flocked to hear him and to be baptized. The authorities took a dim view of this since John, like other prophets before him, brazenly neglected to mention rules and rituals and tithing. Instead, he stressed such things as generosity and honesty toward one's fellow human beings.

Even worse, he failed to mention the Judeans' special status as sons of Abraham. Indeed, when some of the authorities confronted him, he showed utter contempt for any such notion of group morality. "Abraham's descendants?" he exclaimed, pointing to the rocks and pebbles strewn along the banks of the Jordan. "Let me tell you, God could turn these countless stones into descendants of Abraham. The day is already upon us," he added, "when all persons will be judged not on what group they belong to, but on how they show their love for God and for one another." The authorities wanted to clap him in jail for such heresy, but the size of his following gave them pause.

It was in association with this unruly nuisance that Jesus began his public life. If he was looking for a way to get off on the wrong foot with the authorities, he found it.

He also had something else working against him: he wasn't a Judean. He was a native of Galilee, a province in northern Palestine, where the people were less fundamentalist. Galileans were suspiciously liberal, even lax, by the rigid standards of Judean authorities. They were not in such bad odor as the incorrigible people of Samaria (a province between Galilee and Judea thoroughly contaminated by infidel ideas), but their generally low level of intolerance was highly unorthodox.

They were not apathetic, however. They were interested in John's crusade, and not a few of them made the inconvenient trip into Judea to hear what he had to say. Among these was Jesus; however, he was different, for John was expecting him.

One of the things that John had to say was that he was merely the forerunner of someone else, someone much more important than he. When asked if he himself might be the Messiah, he replied obliquely but forcefully in the negative. "I baptize you with water," he said, "but the one who is to come after me will baptize you with the spirit of God. I'm not worthy even to loosen his sandals."

What he meant was not exactly clear, of course, probably not even to him. But when Jesus appeared among the crowd at the Jordan River and asked to be baptized, John evidently sensed that this was no ordinary request or requester. "I should be baptized by you," he protested. "Why have you come to me?" Jesus quietly insisted, however, that it was the proper thing to do, and John baptized him. And Jesus felt God's love—a Father's love—suffuse his being, and he knew that his mission had begun.

Temptation

After this experience, Jesus needed to be alone. He left the crowded riverbank and took refuge in the dry, uncultivated countryside. For six long weeks he kept to himself, eating and drinking only enough to keep himself alive. We can surmise that his thoughts were long and serious, and that he was troubled and uneasy. As for any unique spark of divinity within him, just what it was and just how it affected his humanity, we cannot know. In his vision at the river, God had called him "my beloved Son." If, indeed, he had been chosen to rescue the Jewish people from the authorities now stifling them, what burdens, what dangers, what personal suffering lay ahead? And what powers could he call upon to meet the awesome challenge?

Alone out there in the desert, weakened by his fasting and his anxiety, he was tempted to put his Father to the test. Could he turn the desert rocks around him into loaves of bread? Could he go into Jerusalem and, in sight of the crowds, fling himself from a temple tower and let his Father waft him safely—and spectacularly—to the ground? Could he perhaps use his Father's power, as some Jewish heroes had done in a limited way, to bring the nations of the world under his dominion? As these thoughts crossed his mind, he spurned them. It wasn't for him to test his Father. If anything, it was his Father who was testing him. His mission was not to impose his will on others but to win their hearts and minds. That would be the hardest thing of all.

The First Disciples

On his return to the Jordan, Jesus found some reason for encouragement. This time John was more explicit, revealing that he had shared in the vision of God's special love for Jesus, identifying him as "the one who is to come after me," and welcoming him as the Son of God. The title was impressive, if imprecise; the sons of Abraham also considered themselves to be sons of God, but was this *the* Son of God?

The title was impressive enough—or perhaps Jesus himself was impressive enough—for two of John's disciples to follow Jesus as he left. After a few moments Jesus turned back to them and asked what they wanted.

"Where do you live?" one of them asked him.

"Come along with me," he answered genially, "and you'll see."

They spent the rest of the day with him. There's no record of their conversation, but that night one of the two, named Andrew, went to his brother Simon and asked him to come and meet the Messiah. Simon agreed, and, as the two brothers entered the rooms where Jesus was staying, Jesus greeted Simon by name. Then, apparently impressed with the solid look of the man, he smiled and added, "We'll call you Peter" (after the Greek word for "rock"). It would be some years before Peter would justify the aptness of that pun.

The next morning Jesus started back to Galilee. On the way he met a man named Philip, who lived in Bethsaida, near the Sea of Galilee, and who evidently was known to Andrew and Peter. Jesus asked Philip to become one of his followers. Philip not only agreed to do so but also sought out a friend, Nathanael, and eagerly reported that he had met the Messiah, the Anointed One, the Christ of whom the prophets had written. Nathanael was skeptical, even cynical. He'd heard of messiahs before. Israel was cluttered with them. Who was this one?

"Jesus," replied Philip, "the son of Joseph of Nazareth."

"Nazareth?" Nathanael countered with a contempt worthy of a temple official. "Can anything good come out of Nazareth?"

There was only one rational response to this, and Philip chose it. "Come and see," he said.

And so Nathanael went and saw—and heard. When Jesus noticed them approaching, he looked at Nathanael and slyly exclaimed, "Well, here comes an honest Israelite!"

"How did you know me?" asked Nathanael, with a vanity doubtless born of innocence.

"Why, I knew you before Philip found you," Jesus replied with as much gravity as he could muster, "when you were sitting under the fig tree."

"Rabbi!" Nathanael cried in astonishment, his cynicism suddenly melting into credulity. "You are indeed the Son of God and the King of Israel as well!"

"You say this because I said that I saw you under the fig tree?" asked Jesus in mock surprise. "You'll see greater things than this. The heavens will open, and the angels of God will be seen about the Son of man."

Water into Wine

Two days later Jesus was back in Galilee, in Cana, Nathanael's hometown. He arrived in time to go with his mother, Mary, to a wedding reception. In Israel at the time, such affairs could last as long as a week, and thus it was no great surprise when, on this occasion, the hapless host ran out of wine. Mary, distressed by the family's embarrassment, reported to her son, "They haven't any more wine."

Jesus sensed a request behind her report, but at first he resisted. After his severe temptation in the Judean desert, he hesitated to put any power he might have to a public test, especially in any matter that even bordered on the frivolous. It was too early to attract attention. "What's that to me?" he protested. "My time has yet to come."

Mary refused to argue. She was his mother and had known him intimately for thirty years. With supreme confidence she simply turned to the servants and asked them to follow his instructions. Caught between the demands of courteous obedience and wary discretion, Jesus chose a middle way—to obey, but as discreetly as possible. He pointed to half a dozen very large, empty jars standing on the floor nearby and asked the servants to fill them with water.

After they had done so, he asked further that they take some samples of the jars' contents to the steward in charge of the refreshments. After tasting the samples, the steward complimented the host on the fine quality of the wine being served so near the end of the reception. "It's customary," he observed, "to serve the good wine first and then, after the well-oiled guests have become less fastidious, to serve the poor wine. But you have held back the good wine till now."

The host, for any of various reasons, may not have been in any condition to understand just what the steward was saying. Nor did the guests or servants, being variously distracted, seem to notice that anything unusual had happened. But some of Jesus' new disciples were there, watching their rabbi more attentively than others, and they were impressed.

First Skirmishes 2

After a few days' rest in Capernaum, a bustling town on the northern shore of the Sea of Galilee where his mother was living at the time, Jesus set out southward again. This time, with some of his friends, he headed for Jerusalem to celebrate the feast of the Passover. More than a thousand years before, when Egypt's firstborn sons had died in a divinely ordained epidemic, the homes of the captive Israelites had been spared or "passed over," and soon thereafter the Israelites had "passed over" from slavery to freedom. Every year since, the Jews had piously celebrated these events.

Arriving in Jerusalem, Jesus dutifully went to the temple. He was shocked by the raucous commercialism of the outer court. Here merchants sold animals to pilgrims for the ritual sacrifices, and money changers sold the special coins required for paying taxes. Behind this feverish activity lurked the temple priests, the Sadducees, who permitted it for a gratifying cut of the profits.

Jesus' shock was profound, his anger overwhelming. For one who had been so diffident at a wedding reception in a remote village, his reaction was startling. He strode about the court like a whirlwind, overturning tables and chairs, knocking over cages of animals and birds, spilling coins onto the pavement. "Get these things out of here!" he shouted at the hastily departing traders. "Stop making my Father's house a marketplace for thieves!"

Jesus' friends, as they watched him in astonishment, recalled a line from the Psalms about the Messiah, "My zeal for your temple will consume me."

Certainly his zeal attracted attention. His behavior in the court had been authoritative, to say the least, and pilgrims who were desperately ill, or lame, or blind, now sought him out and begged to be healed. With the compassionate love that was to become his hallmark, he healed them.

Sure enough, he was soon accosted by angry priests and other temple authorities. Gesturing toward some children who were crowding about him and calling him the Messiah, the authorities asked if he realized what the children were saying. "Certainly," Jesus replied evenly and then added (with a reference to another line from the Psalms), "Haven't you ever read in the Scriptures that out of the mouths of babes comes the truest praise?"

This gave their ulcers a rather nasty turn, and they quickly threw him a challenge. "Can you give us a proof," they demanded, "to show that you have the right to do such things?"

Jesus was not about to play the credentials game with people whose sole interest clearly was not in his credentials—which, for that matter, he had already shown to some extent—but in the protection of their comfortable status quo. And so he toyed with them, though with a very serious answer. "Pull down this temple," he challenged them, "and I'll raise it up again in three days."

Destroying the temple was not quite what they had in mind, and so they retreated for the time being, muttering about a temple that had taken, to date, forty-six years to build. Three days, indeed! The man was a blithering idiot—but dangerous.

As the Gospel of John points out, Jesus was punning again, since the word for "temple" could also refer to the human body. His friends who were there and who heard the remark would not remember it nor understand it until after his death.

Nor would Jesus raise such a commotion in the temple again until the days just before his death.

Nicodemus

The Establishment in Israel was anything but unified. In general, there were three clusters of authorities: the Sadducees, the priests and their fellow functionaries; the Pharisees, a powerful sect of fundamentalists, principally laymen, who insisted on rigorous observance of the letter of religious law and who enjoyed several running theological disputes with the Sadducees; and the Herodians, the civil authorities and lackeys of Rome. No love was lost among them, but they were now fast growing united in their anxiety over Jesus and his growing popularity. He promised to be a radical, a rabble-rouser, a troublemaker, and a threat to all three groups. The sooner he was removed, the better.

However, Nicodemus, a member of the Sanhedrin, the council of assorted authorities that ruled Israel (or tried to), was curious about Jesus, and open-minded enough to try to satisfy his curiosity.

And so, one night soon after the near-riot at the temple, he appeared at Jesus' lodgings. He arrived well after dark, since he had no wish to advertise the meeting. Significantly, he addressed Jesus very respectfully as "Rabbi," explaining that the wonders of healing performed at the temple must mean that Jesus was a teacher sent by God.

Jesus responded to the tribute by simply ignoring it. However, he thereupon drew Nicodemus into one of those mystical discussions that characterize the Gospel of John. "Indeed," he responded, "I must say that unless a person is born again, he cannot see the kingdom of God."

"Born again?" asked Nicodemus. "But how can anyone make a second trip through the womb?"

"Born again not of the body," replied Jesus patiently, "but of water and the Spirit of God. What is born of the body is material, but what is born of the Spirit is spiritual, as invisible and mysterious as the wind."

"How can this be?" asked the puzzled Nicodemus.

Jesus had reason to expect a more sophisticated reaction from a person well versed in their common religion. "You are a teacher here in Israel, yet you don't understand? If you can't believe me when I speak of these earthly things, how will you believe me when I speak of heaven? Moses in the desert lifted the image of a serpent on a pole, so that dying Israelites might look up at it and be cured. Likewise the Son of man must be lifted up, so that those who believe in him may have life forever."

The conversation presumably continued in this vein, but there is no specific record of when or how Nicodemus departed. He was destined to appear twice again in the story.

The Samaritan Woman

During his brief stay in Jerusalem, Jesus almost unintentionally had attracted a following already larger than that of John the Baptist. This may have occurred partly because John had recently been thrown into prison by the uneasy authorities. Not only had he continued to preach his unsufferable heresies, but he also had publicly condemned the illicit marriage of Herod Antipas, the governor of Galilee and its neighbor to the west, Perea. Thus he had attacked Herod's wife as well, for whose fury hell had no equivalent. It was to be the death of him.

The report of John's arrest alarmed Jesus, as did rumors that the Judean Pharisees were planning something similar for him. And so he and his friends discreetly headed north for Galilee. Before long they had left Judea behind them and were trudging the hot and dusty roads of Samaria.

Samaria was not a comfortable route for Jews traveling between Judea and Galilee; indeed, most Jews avoided it by taking a longer eastern route across the Jordan and through Perea. The Samaritans, besides their infidel leanings, centered their Hebraic religion on the temple they had built on Mount Gerizim, and they considered the temple at Jerusalem an impertinence. Thus Jews traveling through Samaria were fair game for religious extremists and other highwaymen. For protection, they generally made the trip in caravans; stragglers and other loners traveled at their own considerable risk. To bring hostility to a fever pitch, it seems, nothing is so effective as what people call religion. Eventually Jesus would be among its many victims.

On this trip, there were a couple of reasons for him to choose to go home through Samaria. One was that the route was so much shorter; another, that he might be in less danger from the people in Samaria than from Herod Antipas & Co. in Perea. Whatever his reasons, he and some of his friends headed north. At about the halfway point they found themselves approaching a Samaritan village called Sychar, not far from Mount Gerizim.

Perhaps out of caution, Jesus decided not to go into the town. Instead, he stopped to rest by a well outside the town while his friends went in to buy some food. It was about noon. He must have felt very frustrated; he was hot and tired and very thirsty, but there was no bucket at the well and thus no water to be had. The temptation to perform a small miracle of convenience must have been very great.

A bucket appeared, however, carried by a woman of the town who had come to draw some water, and Jesus asked her for a drink. Recognizing him as a Jewish pilgrim, she replied in a religious vein, "How can a Jew bring himself to ask for a drink of water from a Samaritan?" Declining to be drawn into a squabble, Jesus simply looked at her thoughtfully. Doubtless with some muttering, the woman dipped her bucket into the well, brought it up, and offered him a drink. And thereupon followed another double-meaning conversation like that with Nicodemus.

Nodding his thanks, Jesus remarked, "If you knew what the power of God can give, and if you could recognize who it is that asked you for a drink, *you* would have asked *me,* and I would have given you living water."

The woman, thinking he meant "running" water, such as one might get from a spring or a stream, accepted the remark as a criticism of the staler well water. The chip had yet to fall from her shoulder. "The well is deep," she replied rather combatively, "and you have nothing to bring up the water with. Where would you get this living water? Do you think yourself greater than Jacob, our ancestor, who gave us this well?"

Jesus avoided any direct comparison. "Whoever drinks this water," he answered quietly, nodding toward the well, "will be thirsty again and again; but whoever drinks the water that I can give will never be thirsty thereafter. Such water can become a spring of eternal life."

If she had been a less practical, down-to-earth type, the woman by now might have caught on that this strange fellow was speaking of something beyond H_2O. Instead, she grew cynical. "I'll have some of that water," she challenged him. "If I'm never thirsty, I won't have to trudge out here for water."

"All right," said Jesus with a wry smile. "Get your husband and bring him here."

"I have no husband," she replied guardedly.

"You put that very well," Jesus countered, looking at her squarely, "since you've had five husbands, and the man you're living with is not your husband."

The woman grinned, quite unabashed but nonetheless impressed. "I see you're a prophet," she commented. Unable to resist the opportunity for a little religious controversy, she added, gesturing toward Mount Gerizim, "We and our ancestors have long worshiped in the temple on this mountain, but you people say that God must be worshiped in Jerusalem."

Jesus sighed. To such distinctions had worship fallen. "Believe me," he said, "the time is near when God will be worshiped neither merely on the mountain nor merely in Jerusalem. We know what we worship better than you: humankind's salvation will come through the Jews. But soon God will be worshiped not in a special place but in spirit and truth. God is Spirit, and his worship must come from the spirit, the love, of the worshiper."

Things were getting a little deep and slippery for the woman, who may have felt a headache coming on. She decided to end the argument as abruptly as she had started it, with a vague appeal to authority. "Well, when the Messiah, the Christ, arrives, he'll explain all such things," she said.

"You're talking to him," Jesus replied. That made her stare for a moment, but just then Jesus' friends appeared, and she turned away and headed back to town.

His friends were surprised to find him talking alone with a woman. It was strictly against regulations for a man to have any conversation with a woman "in the street," even if she was his wife. This particular instance was even worse, since this was a *Samaritan* woman. Although their curiosity must have been almost unbearable, they somehow managed to restrain themselves from asking a question or making a comment. Instead, they offered him something to eat.

Jesus, lost in thought, declined the offer, adding that he had food they didn't know about. His friends were puzzled. Had someone brought him some food? Had he actually *eaten* with that Samaritan? Surely not.

The murmuring brought Jesus out of his reverie, at least partly. "What sustains me," he explained, "is my mission to obey the will of him who sent me, to do the work he has assigned to me." Then, looking out over the fields of ripening grain that lay before them, he added, "The fields have been sown, and you will reap the harvest." His friends stared at the fields, stared at him, and went on with their lunch.

Meanwhile, the woman was back in town urging her neighbors to come out to the well and see the Messiah. This stranger, she solemnly assured them, had told her all about her past life. Soon she reappeared at the well with a large contingent of townspeople. Some came out of curiosity, but others seem to have come because of something more intense.

After listening to him for a while, they invited him and his friends to come into town and stay awhile. He accepted the invitation, and the travelers enjoyed the next two days as guests. By the end of their visit some of the people were acclaiming Jesus as nothing less than the Savior of the world.

"Your Son Will Live"

Jesus' reception when he finally arrived in Galilee was surprisingly cordial. Since many Galileans had been in Jerusalem for the Passover and had already returned, his reputation for wonder working and disruption of the temple bureaucracy had preceded him. Indeed, his reputation for instant healing had burgeoned, so much so that a Herodian bureaucrat, no less, traveled from his home in Capernaum to Jesus in Cana, some twenty miles away, to ask him to come to Capernaum and heal his dying son.

As rumors of the request spread among them, the crowd following Jesus urged him to grant it. With some impatience, Jesus resisted at first. "Unless you see wonders performed," he complained, "you will not believe in me."

His resentment, however, soon softened into compassion. The official himself was guilty of no mere idle curiosity. He was obviously desperate, and he had shown at least enough faith to make the inconvenient trip. Jesus often felt very lonely amid all the misunderstanding, shallow adulation, skepticism, and downright hostility that he encountered, and a little genuine faith would always touch his heart.

The man anxiously repeated his request, "Please, hurry and come, before the boy dies."

"Go on home," Jesus replied. "Your son will live." It was one o'clock in the afternoon.

Showing an increasing faith, the official, instead of remonstrating, turned and headed for home. Perhaps because men of means avoided traveling the unguarded roads after dark, he didn't get to Capernaum until early the next morning. As he approached his home, some of his servants ran out to greet him with the news that his son was rapidly recovering. When, he asked them, had the boy started to get better? "It was yesterday," they replied, "about one o'clock."

The official and his whole household became believers on the spot.

Rejection in Nazareth

Shortly thereafter, Jesus left Cana and walked the short distance to Nazareth, perhaps hoping to find a little rest in his hometown. On the following Sabbath he attended the services at the local synagogue, as had been his practice for many years. Among others, he was asked to read from the Scriptures. When his turn came, he was handed a scroll from the book of the prophet Isaiah. Turning the scroll, he found what he considered an appropriate passage, a prophecy about the Messiah, and read it to the congregation:

> "The Spirit of the Lord is upon me because he has anointed me to
>   bring the good news to the poor,
>   to comfort the broken-hearted,
>   to announce the release of captives,

> to restore sight to the blind,
> to free the oppressed, and
> to proclaim the year of the Lord."

After returning the scroll, he sat down. (It was the custom to stand, in respect, while reading from the Scriptures and to sit while commenting on them.) All eyes were on him. The congregation was very quiet and, indeed, seemed expectant.

"This prophecy," Jesus began, "has now come true." We have no record of the rest of his commentary, although it evidently impressed the congregation very favorably. Indeed, there was some murmuring among them: could this be the Jesus they had known, the son of Joseph the carpenter? How had he developed such eloquence?

But then Jesus changed the subject. "I'm sure," he said, anticipating them, "that you'll ask that I do such things here as happened recently in Capernaum. I can only answer that no prophet is credited at home. Prophets of old—Elijah and Elisha, for instance—worked wonders, not for the people of Israel, but for people in foreign lands, in Sidon and Syria."

It wasn't the most politic thing he could have said. People did not like to be reminded of how shabbily the prophets had been treated, and the congregation was further incensed by Jesus' refusal to put on a faith-healing show for them in Nazareth. The synagogue rang with angry shouts and epithets. Some of the more aggressive worshipers seized Jesus and hauled him outside, carrying him amid the swirling crowd to a nearby cliff, apparently to express their disapproval with the force of gravity. But at the critical moment Jesus slipped from their grasp and, to their consternation, irretrievably melted away.

Fishers of Persons

Having pretty clearly overstayed his welcome, Jesus left Nazareth for Capernaum on a route that took him along the western shore of the Sea of Galilee (known also, more accurately, as Lake Gennesaret; although 680 feet below sea level, it was, and is, a lake). One morning on the way, as he walked along the shore with a crowd of curious people, he noticed a couple of fishing boats that had been beached; and there, standing beside one of them, was Peter the Rock. Jesus, who occasionally seemed in danger of being inadvertently pushed out to sea by the eager crowd, asked Peter who owned the boats.

"This one is mine," Peter replied, gesturing toward the one next to him.

"I'll take it," Jesus grinned. "Would you mind putting out a little way from shore?"

Peter grunted his compliance, and the two of them got into the boat. A dozen yards or so offshore Jesus asked Peter to stop, and Jesus began speaking to the crowd.

When he had finished and the crowd had begun to disperse, he suggested to Peter that he and his fellow fishermen take the boat out to deeper water and do a little fishing.

"We've been working at it all night," grumped Peter, "and we haven't caught a thing." But then he did catch something in Jesus' expression. "However, if you insist, we'll let down our nets." His partners—his brother Andrew, and James and John—joined them in the boat, and out they went. Down went the nets, and up they came, filled to the breaking point with suddenly cooperative fish. Soon their boat and the other, which had joined them, were so full of fish that they were in danger of sinking. Peter knelt before Jesus in the floundering boat and cried in alarm, "Leave me, Lord, for I am a sinful man!" But Jesus reassured him that all would be well.

They managed to get ashore safely enough and to dispose of the fish, but Peter, Andrew, James, and John left at once to accompany Jesus to Capernaum. "From now on," Jesus told them as they headed north, "you will be fishers of persons."

A Sabbath in Capernaum

Despite his unnerving experience in Nazareth, on the following Sabbath Jesus attended the synagogue service in Capernaum and spoke before the congregation. This time his remarks were less inflammatory but evidently were forceful enough for the congregation to comment among themselves on the authority that his words seemed to carry. His message had a direct, personal quality that they had not detected in the divisive institutional authority of their usual teachers.

The service was interrupted, however, when a psychotic in the congregation suddenly went into a frenzy and screamed at Jesus, "What is it you want, Jesus of Nazareth? Have you come to destroy me and my friends? I know you; you are the holy messenger of God!"

"Silence!" Jesus commanded in a loud voice. "This man must be left in peace!"

The unfortunate fellow immediately stopped his screaming and, after suffering a convulsion, became very quiet and passive. The congregation stared at him in astonishment. The demon that had possessed him had cravenly departed, driven away by this eloquent and mysterious fellow from Nazareth.

The news soon spread far and wide. It reached the authorities, who welcomed it, though uneasily. Healing could be classified as a kind of work and, thus, as forbidden on the Sabbath. Here was something that they might be able to use against Jesus, if necessary. Of course, they'd be happier if he'd just go away.

From the synagogue Jesus went to Peter's home. Peter's motives in extending the invitation were mixed, it seems. His mother-in-law was sick in bed with a fever; it would be convenient, he suggested, if she were up and about. Jesus conceded the point; on their arrival he went to the woman at once and ordered that the fever leave her. It did, and soon she was bustling about, preparing a meal for her obliging guest and his friends. That evening neighbors dropped in with sick relatives and friends, and her guest continued to oblige for several hours. Since the sun had set, bringing the end of the Jewish day, the rules against compassion no longer applied.

"Your Sins Are Forgiven"

Next morning Jesus rose early and walked out to the desert to be alone and pray. After all the bustle and pressing demands in the crowded house the evening before, the desert in the early morning offered cool, clear air and quiet solitude for lifting one's mind and heart to God without institutional assistance. Here he could gather strength and resolve for whatever lay ahead.

He was soon found, however, by some of the villagers who, with Peter, had come out looking for him. Soon a crowd began to gather about him, asking him to return. But he declined their invitation. "I must bring the Good News of the kingdom of God to other towns," he explained gently. "That is why God has sent me."

Thus Jesus began an extended tour of the towns of Galilee, preaching the Good News in synagogues and village squares. He brought a message of love and hope, especially to the sick. People with all kinds of ailments and diseases pressed about him constantly, many meeting him as he came into a town, fewer trailing him as he left.

In one town, for instance, a wide lane suddenly opened in the crowd, the people drawing back in fright as a leper approached. This leper proved pathetically hesitant, too diffident to make a direct request. "If you wish it, sir," he said to Jesus, "you can make me clean."

Jesus' response was, characteristically, unsentimental but compassionate—and immediate. "I do wish it," he replied, reaching out and touching the man. "May you be made clean." And the man was healed on the spot.

He was, however, still ritually unclean, and Jesus felt that he should observe the amenities. "Before you advertise this," he warned, "show your new condition to the priest appointed for such duties and make the offering prescribed by Moses." Only in this way could the man be accepted back into normal society.

Despite his caution, reports of the cure quickly spread throughout the community. The crowds grew enormous and hard to handle. He preached and healed until, exhausted, he fled again to the desert to seek relief and renewal in solitary prayer. His attempt at escape was not very successful, however. The most enterprising of the petitioners found him, and he could not say them nay.

A few days later he was back in Capernaum. The inevitable crowd swarming around him presented a less than edifying spectacle. The endless jockeying for places near the healer was highly competitive; so that, ironically, those most fit and least in need of a cure were the ones most likely to reach the choicest spots. One day, indeed, a young man so badly paralyzed as to be permanently bedridden was brought on a litter by four good friends to the edge of the crowd, only to find that they could get no closer. Having brought him this far, the four friends were not about to turn back. With an improvising spirit born of desperation, they decided on a bypass route. Skirting the crowd, they found a spot where they could maneuver the litter to the roof of the house. This done, they located the room where Jesus was, opened a hole in the roof, and lowered their burden to the floor.

The entry was spectacular enough to distract Jesus and even to cause a lull in the competitive supplications engulfing him. He looked at the paralytic and then up at his determined friends, shaking his head in appreciation of their undauntable faith. "My son," he said to the young man lying on his litter, "your sins are forgiven." Although the sick man hadn't expected this, he brightened up considerably, for it was common knowledge that forgiveness of one's sins would bring healing.

As Jesus' reputation and popularity had kept growing, so had the uneasiness of the authorities. The crowds that followed him now usually included their representatives, such as Sadducees, Pharisees, and law experts usually called "scribes." We have no explicit explanation of their motives, but it's not hard to infer that they were up to no good. As we might put it today, they were taking notes. Their questions were often tricky and almost always hostile, and they would later use Jesus' answers as evidence against him in his mock trial.

On this occasion some scribes and Pharisees, sitting in the room as "observers," pricked up their ears at Jesus' statement that the paralytic's sins were forgiven. This was an intolerable presumption, an infuriating piece of effrontery, for no one could forgive sins but God. From another viewpoint, too, it was a cheap shot, since anyone could *say* that the man's sins were forgiven, and how could anyone else prove otherwise? The more they thought about it and murmured about it among themselves, the more affronted they felt.

It is probably significant that, according to the record, they kept their objections to themselves. Jesus, however, sensing their unrest, answered them directly on both points. "Why do you raise such questions?" he asked them, doubtless to their further consternation. "Do you think it's easier to say, 'Your sins are forgiven' than to say, 'Take up your bed and walk'? It seems I must show you that the Son of man has the authority here on earth to forgive sins."

By now he had everyone's attention. An expectant hush settled over the fidgety crowd. Turning to the paralytic, he ordered, "Get up. Take your litter and go home." Only too happy to oblige, the man got up, gathered together his litter, signaled ecstatically to his friends overhead, and left the house. This time the crowd made way for him.

After a moment, while the authorities sat staring at the floor in glum chagrin, the people began discussing the incident. "Well," said a man to his companion, "we've seen some mighty wonderful things here today."

Pious Disapproval

Shortly thereafter, Jesus took a walk down to the shore of the lake. He surely had more reason than most of us to "get out of the house" now and then. People followed him, of course, but at least he had some room to breathe and some fresher air.

As he was returning home, he noticed a tax collector sitting in his roadside office. He knew that such men, who collected taxes for the Roman occupiers plus generous fees for themselves, were considered ritually unclean by pious Jews because they consorted with pagans. Indeed, they were cordially hated as a group, especially by the religious authorities: tax money was life's blood to officialdom, which deeply resented any heathen bloodletting. Despite this, or because of it, Jesus called to the tax collector, "Come, follow me." The man (who evidently was Matthew, the apostle-to-be) gathered up his coins and papers and joined the strolling group.

In fact, he went further, inviting Jesus and his closest friends to a dinner party at his house. Jesus accepted the invitation. Among the guests were some other tax collectors and other disreputable types, and this disturbed the ever-watchful authorities. After dinner, therefore, as Jesus and his friends were on their way home, they were accosted by a few Pharisees, complete with attendant scribes, and accused of associating with tax collectors and other sinners.

As usual, Jesus was ready for them, answering their objection but refusing to take these self-righteous busybodies seriously. "It's not the healthy who need a doctor," he replied evenly, "but the sick. My mission is not to the righteous"—he restrained himself from inserting *such as yourselves*—"but to sinners." Like so many of his answers to their challenges, this one was logical enough yet oblique enough to leave them speechless—not satisfied by any means but, for the moment, speechless.

The Pharisees were not the only purse-lipped group in Israel at the time. There were also the Essenes, a resolutely ascetic band who lived withdrawn, frugal lives in the stony hills (and who left us the Dead Sea Scrolls). And there were the followers of John the Baptist, who could purse their lips with the best of them. They were much devoted to fasting—to individual fasting, that is, far beyond the requirements of the Law. One day some of the Baptist's followers, being in the neighborhood, took the opportunity to point out to Jesus, with some asperity, that the Pharisees and John's disciples did a great deal of fasting, yet Jesus and his disciples did not.

Jesus may have been very disappointed in them. He and John together had announced the coming of the kingdom of God, the overturning of the reign of fear and sorrow by the reign of love and joy. Yet here they were, demanding adherence by others to old customs that they preferred for themselves. His answer was gentle and good-humored but uncompromising.

"Do wedding guests fast," he asked them rhetorically, "while the bridegroom is still in their company? They can do their fasting after he is gone."

"No one patches old clothing with a piece of new cloth," he continued, hoping to emphasize the radical nature of his mission, the radical difference between the old reign and the new. "The new cloth would be too strong and tight, and the old cloth would simply tear again. Likewise, no one stores freshly made wine in old, dry wineskins, lest the fermenting wine burst them. New wine belongs in new, elastic wineskins."

Not long after the encounter with John's disciples, Jesus and his friends visited Jerusalem for a religious festival. One day during their visit, Jesus stopped at a famous healing pool called *Bethesda* in

Hebrew. On the five porches built around the pool, a large number of people with a variety of ailments waited patiently. The story was that an angel of the Lord visited the pool now and then to stir up the water, although the disturbance may have been caused by sudden spurts in the flow of water from the spring. In any case, the water was thought to have healing powers when disturbed, but only briefly, so that the first person to step into the water after it had been stirred would be healed, and the runners-up would not. Despite this frustrating limitation, the pool apparently was always crowded.

It might be expected that the porches would contain some pitiful cases and that Jesus would be attracted to such cases. One man, he was told, had been there for thirty-eight years. He went to this man immediately and was shocked by his look of hopeless apathy as he lay stretched out on a straw mat on the floor of the porch. Bending over him, Jesus asked, "Do you want to be made well?"

The man stared up at him through glazed eyes. "Sir," he explained, "I haven't anyone to help me to the pool when the water becomes disturbed, and so someone else always gets there ahead of me."

"Get up," replied Jesus, straightening and stepping back. "Take up your mat and walk."

Obediently the man got to his feet, rolled up his mat, and walked away. Jesus left, too, to get out of the crowd.

The cured man, it turned out, was hurrying away to the temple, presumably to make the offerings demanded by ritual. When he arrived there, still carrying his mat, some authorities stopped him to point out that, since it was the Sabbath, carrying the mat around was against the law.

"But," he protested, "the man who healed me told me to take up my mat and walk."

"Oh?" Evidently they smelled bigger game than this unprepossessing fellow. "And who was it who healed you?"

"I don't know his name," he answered. Shrugging helplessly, they let him go.

He learned the name a little later, however, when Jesus met him at the temple and, after congratulating him on his obvious good health, warned him against losing it again by sinning. The man then hied himself to the authorities and identified Jesus as the man who had healed him. And they sought Jesus out and charged him with doing healing work on the Sabbath.

"My Father works unceasingly," Jesus answered them, "and so must I."

The authorities stared at one another in shocked dismay. The man was outrageous. He seemed to be saying not only that he was equal to God but also that he was even independent of God—or, more to the point, of *them*. Jesus hastened to set them as straight as he could on such a subject. At least he might correct some misconceptions. He could not, however, explain his relationship with the Father.

"Let me assure you," he began, "that the Son does nothing by himself but simply imitates the Father. The Father loves the Son and reveals his work to him, and more marvelous things are yet in store for you to wonder at. As the Father brings the dead to life, so can the Son. And to the Son the Father has delegated the judgment of humankind, so that all may honor the Son as they honor the Father. Whoever fails to honor the Son fails also to honor the Father who sent him.

"I tell you truly, whoever accepts my message and believes in him who sent me already has passed the judgment into eternal life. The time is coming, and indeed has already begun, when the spiritually dead will hear the voice of the Son of God and live. The Father has the power of life and has given it to the Son, as he has given him the right of judgment as the Son of man. You needn't be surprised; there will be a time when the dead will hear him and arise, those who have led good lives will be vindicated, others will be condemned. I can do nothing on my own. My judgment is right only because I am governed by him who sent me."

"As for testimony," he continued, but on another related subject, "it's pointless for me to testify on my own behalf. You've heard John's testimony, and it's the truth. But the real testimony is that of my Father, in the works that he has given me to perform to show that he has sent me. Yet you won't accept his word or believe in his messenger. You search the Scriptures for the way to eternal life; those very Scriptures tell you about me, yet you will not accept me as the way to that life.

"I want no earthly glory. But I see no love of God in you because I have come in my Father's name, yet you will not accept me. (If someone else came in his own name, him, I suppose, you'd accept!) You accept the testimony of persons, but what of God's? Reject that, and how can you have any belief? Not I but Moses, the very source of all your hopes, will accuse you before the Father. If you really believed Moses, who wrote about me, you would now believe me. But if you won't accept his word, how can you accept mine?"

Evidently this discourse went unanswered. The authorities were looking for servile conformity, and instead he was giving them hard questions. They would have to take him on again some other day.

Indeed, these aggressive bureaucrats seemed to operate in relay teams, dogging Jesus' footsteps wherever he might go, watching and waiting, ready to pounce. They showed a special fondness for stalking him on Sabbath days, since it was on the Sabbath that even ordinary living under the law became precarious. Unless one remained deliberately catatonic throughout the day, it was hard not to break some rule or other amid the confining thicket.

One Sabbath day, for instance, Jesus and his friends were walking through a wheat field on their way from one town to another. Some in the group were hungry enough to pick the heads off the wheat and eat a few kernels of grain. Thus, at least technically, they broke two rules governing conduct on the Sabbath: picking the wheat was a kind of reaping, and rubbing the heads in their hands to release the kernels was a kind of threshing, and both reaping and threshing were forbidden.

Sure enough, even on a casual stroll through a wheat field they were subject to the gimlet eye and the censorious tongue. "Look at that!" an excited gaggle of Pharisees cried to Jesus. "Your followers are breaking the Sabbath law!"

Jesus shook his head. Didn't these people have anything better to do? Did they really deserve a serious answer?

"Surely you've read the story about King David," he replied. "When he and some of his retinue grew hungry one Sabbath day, they went into the house of God and ate some of the ceremonial bread reserved by law for the priests. Indeed, the priests themselves do temple work on the Sabbath, and this isn't considered sinful.

"You see before you someone who is more important than the temple. If you understood that passage in the Scriptures, 'I want to see kindness to others, not ritual sacrifices,' you'd be less free with your condemnations. The Sabbath was made for man, not man for the Sabbath. And the Son of man is master of the Sabbath."

The Pharisees were used to arguing fine points of the law and discussing various interpretations in exhausting detail. A sweeping response like this simply left them agape. It also left them feeling very insecure, since any such viewpoint, if widely accepted, would undermine their profession, their position in society, their very reason for being what they were. This did not bode well for Jesus, since there are few things more dangerous than insecure authorities.

The next confrontation was more direct. When Jesus arrived in town, he and his friends went to the local synagogue, where a man whose right arm had become paralyzed and useless came up to him. (An apocryphal gospel adds that the man explained to Jesus that he could no longer work in his trade of mason and would soon become a beggar.) Jesus, aware that his every move was being watched by a nearby cluster of authorities, grew angry with their indifference to the fellow's plight. Eyes flashing, he addressed them directly.

"Who among you," he challenged them, "would not, on the Sabbath, save a sheep that had fallen into a pit? Isn't a man more valuable than a sheep? I ask you, is it lawful on the Sabbath to do good, or must one do harm by failing to do good?"

Their only reply was silence. Clearly they were now more eager to see him deliberately break the law than to discuss the matter. And so he obliged them. "Hold out your hand," he said to the man, who immediately stretched his right arm out in front of him and exercised the fingers rapturously.

Later that day some leading Pharisees held a meeting, attended by some equally insecure Herodians, to discuss stronger ways of dealing with Jesus. They had to find a way to discredit this troublemaker, at the very least, or, preferably, to get rid of him altogether.

Fall of an Ally 3

When Jesus got wind of the authorities' unfriendly scheming, he left town for the relative safety of the lakeshore. A large crowd surged and jostled behind him, growing formidably, it seemed, with every step. The crowds generally, in fact, were now being rapidly augmented by hordes from all over Palestine and even from the pagan cities within and around it. The pagan element was large enough to remind Matthew the evangelist of a prophecy by Isaiah that the Messiah would be the hope of the Gentiles.

Perhaps because the situation was obviously becoming too much for any single person to handle, at one point during this period Jesus withdrew to a nearby hill with a select group of disciples and chose twelve of them to stay with him and join actively in his mission. Included were Peter, James, and John, and a fellow by the name of Judas.

The Sermon on the Mount

On their way down the hillside this select group was met by a throng of disciples impatiently waiting for Jesus to return. After stopping to sit on a sloping hillock where he could look out over the gathering, he asked them to sit down, too, and make themselves as comfortable as possible. Then he launched into one of the most famous discourses in history. As usual, he did not talk down to his audience, much less to its lowest common denominator. If what he had to say was puzzling at times, well, maybe it was worth some sober second thoughts.

"The poor and forlorn are blessed," he began, "because the

kingdom of heaven will be theirs. Those who hunger for justice will be satisfied, and those who weep will have joy. Blessed, too, are the humble in mind, who will inherit the earth; the merciful, who will receive mercy; the pure in heart, who will see God; and the peacemakers, whom God will love as his sons. And you, my friends, will be blessed when you are persecuted and condemned and made outcasts in the name of righteousness for my sake, because this is how the prophets were treated, and you will be richly rewarded in heaven.

"Stay true to your mission: you are the salt that will flavor the world, and if the salt itself loses its flavor, what is there that can restore it? You are the light to brighten the world. Don't hide that light timidly under a pail, but let it shine out so that others may see the good you do and honor your Father in heaven.

"Respect his law and the words of his prophets. I have come not to cancel them out but to carry them to fulfillment. God's law will endure, in every detail, till the end of time. Whoever disobeys the most minor of his commandments and teaches others to do so, will rank least in the kingdom of heaven, but whoever obeys and teaches obedience will rank very high. Let me assure you, righteousness like that of the scribes and Pharisees will never get you into the kingdom of heaven.

"You have heard God's command against murder, but I tell you that it also condemns violent, unjust anger or contempt. If you are making an offering at God's altar and remember an injustice done to your brother, leave the altar, go to your brother and be reconciled, and *then* come back and make your offering. You must take the initiative. Do not neglect God as you might a creditor, or you will have to pay every last penny.

"You have heard God's command against adultery, but I tell you that lustful desire is equally forbidden. If your eye or hand threaten to lead you into sin, its destruction would be better than the risk of hell.

"It has been said in the past that a divorce requires a written certificate. But I tell you that a man who, even with a certificate, divorces a wife who has not been unfaithful is responsible for her adultery if she marries again, and the man who marries her commits adultery.

"You know of the ancient law against breaking an oath sworn before God, but I advise you to leave off swearing altogether. For you, the ideal should be a simple 'yes' or 'no.' Anything beyond this is a compromise with the dishonesty in the world.

"You know the law of retaliation: an eye for an eye, a tooth for a tooth. But I tell you it is better to love your enemies, to return love for hostility or indifference, to bless those who curse you, to pray for those who do you injury. If someone slaps you on the cheek, turn the other to him. If someone steals your overcoat, offer him your jacket as well. Give freely, and don't insist on a return.

"You have heard the counsel to love your neighbors, your relatives and friends, but I tell you it is still better to love your enemies as well. If you befriend only those who would befriend you, what's so good about that? That's something anyone can do, including the godless. But if you befriend someone who would harm you, then will you be greatly rewarded by your Father, who lets his sun shine and his rain fall for the benefit of both his friends and his enemies. Strive to be as generous as he is and, indeed, as perfect as he is.

"But don't make a great show of it, angling for worldly praise, which could cancel any reward from your Father in heaven. When you give alms, don't advertise your virtue by blowing a horn like a hypocrite. Your left hand needn't know what generous things your right hand is doing, but your Father will know and will reward you.

"Likewise, when you pray, don't display your piety to the public at large, but pray quietly to your Father, who can hear your most secret thoughts and who knows what you need even before you ask him. Pray to him like this: 'Our Father in heaven, may your name be kept holy, your kingdom be realized, and your will be done on earth as in heaven. Give us our bread for today. Forgive us our offenses, as we forgive those who offend against us. Do not let us fall into temptation, and preserve us from evil.' If you forgive those who injure you, just so will your Father forgive you. If you do not forgive, neither will your Father.

"So, too, when you fast, don't make a lugubrious display of it. Keep it to yourself. Your Father will see it.

"Beware of accumulating the things of this world, things that can be destroyed by moths and worms and stolen by thieves. Instead, build up a treasure in heaven that will be neither destroyed nor stolen. For where your treasure lies, there will your heart lie also.

"No one can be completely devoted both to God and to personal possessions. Don't grow absorbed in the details of living, in what you eat and drink and wear. Consider the birds who sow no seeds, reap no harvests, store no food in barns. Your Father feeds them, and aren't you more important than they are? Can worry make you grow any taller or live any longer? If you concern yourself with clothes, consider the flowers that grow wild in the field. They neither weave nor sew, yet not even Solomon in all his magnificence was clothed as splendidly as they are. Surely if God so beautifully clothes the fleeting grass, he will do as much as if not more than that for you.

"Absorption in food and drink and clothing—leave it to the godless. Your Father is aware of your needs. Turn your minds rather to him, to his kingdom and his justice, and what you need will be given to you. Don't fret about tomorrow. Let tomorrow do its own worrying. Today's troubles will do well enough till then.

"Don't be eager to condemn the behavior of others lest your own be likewise condemned. Remember generosity: as you measure it out to others, so will it be measured out to you. Don't meddle; can the blind lead the blind? Can you see to remove a splinter from another's eye when the plank it came from is lodged in your own? You had better remove the plank before trying for the splinter. And anyway, your efforts to reform others may well prove futile: why waste your pearls of wisdom on unappreciative swine?

"Ask, and you will be satisfied. Knock, and the door will be opened. Whoever so petitions will receive a response. What father, if his son asks for bread, will give him a stone? If you, with your imperfect love, will care for your children, how much more generously will your heavenly Father care for you! As you would have others deal generously with you, deal likewise with them—this is the counsel of God's law and his prophets.

"Choose the narrow gate. The wide gate leads to perdition, and multitudes pass through it. The path and the gate to eternal life are narrow and are found by few.

"Beware of false prophets. They are wolves in sheep's clothing, but their deeds will reveal them. Brambles do not yield grapes, nor do thistles produce figs. So with prophets: by their fruits you will know them.

"Those who offer me pious flattery—'Lord, Lord,' they cry—will not thereby enter the kingdom, but rather those who obey my heavenly Father. Those who hear my teaching and act on it are building their houses on rocks, to withstand storm and flood; but those who hear my teaching and fail to act on it are building their houses on sand, and the flood will wash them away."

With this, Jesus brought his long discourse to an end. Much of it echoed the Jewish Scriptures, but not those parts that the people were used to hearing about in synagogue and temple. There on the hillside, out in the open, the message was like a breath of fresh air.

The Officer's Servant

On his return to Capernaum, Jesus was met near the city gate by a small group of Jewish elders. A servant of a Roman military officer in the town, they told him, was dying. The officer was very much attached to the servant and had asked them to act as delegates to Jesus. The officer was very sensitive to Jewish xenophobia and thus very diffident about dealing with Jesus directly. However, he had been very generous to the Jewish community, they said, even to the extent of building a synagogue. He deserved generosity in return.

Jesus was impressed. "Very well," he replied to the delegation, "lead the way, and I'll come with you." But as they approached the officer's house, some of his friends came out with a message from him. Knowing that Jews considered the pagan house and its occupants "unclean" and contaminating, they explained, he would not go so far as to ask Jesus to enter it. Just as he himself had the authority to tell others where to go and what to do, so, he was sure, did Jesus have the authority "simply to say the word, and my servant will be healed."

Whatever Jesus may have thought of the officer's diffidence, he was moved by his faith. Throughout his public life Jesus stressed the importance of a petitioner's faith, as though he couldn't exercise any power without it. In this instance he turned to the crowd about him. "Now, *this* is faith!" he exclaimed to them. And then he said rather wistfully, "I have seen nothing like it from Israel."

Nodding encouragingly to the officer's friends, he motioned them to return to the house, which they did. Needless to add, they found the servant fully recovered.

The Widow's Son

One day not long after the healing of the officer's servant, Jesus found himself in the village called Nain. Just outside the city gate he and the crowd with him stepped aside for a funeral procession on its way to the cemetery. A young man had died, he soon learned, leaving his mother, a widow, quite alone in the world. As the bier passed by, Jesus could see the mother following it on the arm of a friend, looking very forlorn and pitiable. And he was touched to the heart.

Yet he was hesitant about bringing anyone back to life. To do so, he knew, would create quite a stir and probably invite some unwelcome attention from the authorities, or at least aggravate their menacing insecurity. But, as he watched the woman going by, his pity overcame his caution. He made his way to her side and spoke to her gently. "You need not mourn," he said.

She stared at him, uncomprehending. He stepped to the bier and touched it, and the procession halted. "Young man," he called out in a loud voice, "I order you, get up!" Amid a chorus of intakes of breath, the young man opened his eyes, lifted himself on his elbows, and stared groggily about him. After the pallbearers had laid their burden down, he struggled to his feet. Jesus stretched out his hand, helped him get his bearings, and led him to his mother.

Whatever the mother's reaction, that of the mourners and the rest of the crowd was about what Jesus had expected. Amid the hubbub, many raised their hands in prayer, loudly thanking God for visiting their village and sending them so great a prophet. And reports of the incident soon were spreading about the village and throughout the surrounding countryside—and into the keen ears of the authorities.

The Baptist's Farewell

While John was in prison, he sent a couple of his disciples to Jesus with a question that must have seemed downright offensive.

"Are you really the one who John said would come after him," they asked, "or should we look for another?"

A mere "yes" would hardly have been a very persuasive answer. "Go back to John," Jesus replied, "and tell him what you've seen and what others have reported to you: that the blind are made to see, the deaf to hear, the lame to walk. Lepers are healed, the dead are brought to life, and the Good News about the kingdom of God is preached to the poor and downtrodden. Surely a reasonable man won't consider my performance an *obstacle* to his belief."

The two emissaries, apparently satisfied, bade him farewell and left. Jesus turned to those crowding about him.

"Why did you go out into the countryside when John was preaching there?" he asked them with a glint in his eyes. "To see a reed bending in the wind? What did you expect? To see a man dressed in velvet, like a courtier? Or did you go out to see a prophet? Well, that is what you saw, and more. As the prophet Malachi predicted, John was sent to make things ready, to prepare the way.

"I assure you, there has never been anyone greater than John until now, for the humblest participant in the kingdom of God can be greater than he. Many believed in the message he brought from God and were baptized. But these were ordinary people, including even tax collectors. The authorities rejected his message, although anyone with ears could hear it.

"They're hard to satisfy. Like petulant children invited to join in one game and then in another, they can always find some objection. They objected to John, with his fasting and abstinence, and charged him with being possessed. Then the Son of man arrived, enjoying his food and drink, and they accused him of being a glutton and a tippler and of hobnobbing with disreputable characters. But the people understand.

"Towns in Israel have followed their leaders in refusing to hear the Good News. The judgment will be harder on them than on pagan towns. I thank God that the message is reaching not the scholarly and proud but the ignorant and humble. The Father knows the Son and is known by the Son—and by those to whom the Son reveals him.

"To whoever finds life under the authorities a joyless burden, I offer some relief. Take my message to heart. Compared to your authorities, I am gentle and undemanding, and the burden I impose is light."

Love and Forgiveness

On rare occasions Jesus was invited to dinner by a Pharisee who, at the moment, happened to be friendlier, or less hostile, than his colleagues. Dinner invitations in Israel at the time seem to have been very frequent and quite casual, often resulting not in what we today would call a dinner party, but rather in a small and rather disorganized public festival, with people coming and going as hunger and social needs might dictate.

It was customary for a host to give a respected guest a kiss of welcome, a bowl of water and a cloth for cleaning off dust-encrusted feet, and some perfumed oil for making them more presentable. On this particular occasion Jesus' host neglected these amenities. He may have overlooked them in the confusion, or he may have been reluctant to show all that much respect to an itinerant preacher of doubtful social status. Whatever the reason, Jesus obviously began his meal—people generally reclined at table, Roman style—with his feet still unattended to.

But at that moment an overwrought woman appeared and rushed over to Jesus. Kneeling by his outstretched feet, she bathed them in a copious flow of tears, wiped them dry with her long, lustrous hair, and kissed them tenderly. Then, producing a small vial, she gently massaged them with a perfumed ointment.

Even at a dinner in first-century Israel, such a performance was unusual enough to attract attention and, of course, cause comment. Much of the comment was of the clucking variety, since the woman had a thoroughly scandalous reputation.

The host was shocked. It was clear to him now that this fellow couldn't be a prophet, or he would have known what kind of woman this was and would have given her short shrift. Ironically, although the censorious Pharisee didn't realize it, Jesus, in a sense, was doing precisely that.

"My friend," said Jesus, divining his host's disapproval and beckoning to him, "may I ask you something?"

"Certainly, Rabbi," replied his host with elaborate civility.

"Let's suppose," said Jesus, with an ill-suppressed twinkle, "that a moneylender forgave two of his debtors all they owed him, one twice as much as the other. Which of the two would be more grateful; which one would love him more?"

The Pharisee turned the question over in his mind for a moment with more solemnity than it deserved. For Pharisees, solemnity was an occupational disease. "I suppose," he finally concluded, "the one whom he forgave the greater amount."

"True enough," Jesus agreed with somewhat less solemnity. "Now as for this woman—when I arrived, you gave me no kiss of greeting, no water for my feet. But she has washed and wiped my feet clean and kissed them most respectfully and made them comfortable with ointment. However many her sins, they are forgiven because she has shown, and thus will receive, much love. In contrast"—looking squarely at his host—"a little love and a little forgiveness go together."

He turned to the woman, who by now was growing calmer. "Indeed, your sins are forgiven." The table buzzed with cynicism: Who does this fellow think he is, forgiving sins? But Jesus continued speaking to the woman. "Your faith has saved you," he assured her. "You may leave in peace." She did.

Whatever may have been the case with this particular woman, Jesus and his message clearly were attractive to many women. Some of them, having independent minds and some independent wealth, assisted Jesus and his twelve apostles with funds. One was called Mary Magdalene, and another was the wife of Herod's chief steward.

The Devil's Advocates

Dinner parties were not a way of life with Jesus, of course. Sometimes he would forget about food, and sometimes his eager audience would crowd about him so tightly and stay so long that he would be in danger of near starvation. They had an advantage over him, since they could leave individually to get some refreshment without being particularly noticed.

One day a house in which he was preaching was so closely packed that, according to Mark, no food could have been eaten, much less served. Some of Jesus' friends considered the situation outrageous and thought that he must be out of his mind to tolerate it. They even worked out a plan to rescue him, but apparently they didn't have to put it into operation.

At any rate, he was busily engaged in another debate with the authorities, whose latest charge was that his power to heal, and especially to heal the "possessed," came from the prince of demons. As a public accusation in an age much taken with demons, the charge had to be answered seriously, and Jesus did answer it as seriously as he could. Yet, as happened so often in his arguments with the authorities, he seems deliberately to have made his response curiously oblique, leaving his benighted hecklers in a state of frustrated bewilderment, which further aggravated their anxious hostility. The authorities had their exorcists and faith healers who had their successes and failures. But Jesus' cures had the reputation of being far more numerous, more spectacular, and more reliable. The authorities, evidently unable to deny that the cures were taking place, now were trying to discredit them by ascribing them to Satan. Jesus' response essentially was that the prince of hate would certainly grant no such powers to someone whose sole purpose in life was to introduce a kingdom of love. And if disease were caused by demons, the minions of Satan, why would Satan help to eradicate them? His function was to cause disease, not cure it. He'd be working at cross purposes.

"A kingdom divided within itself cannot last," he answered his antagonists. "If Satan's kingdom were so divided, it wouldn't have lasted as long as it has. If he is the source of my cures, then who is the source of yours? Or consider the converse: if God is the source of my cures, then so must he be of yours.

"Satan is like a fully armed man guarding his house; he must be overpowered before the house and its contents can be taken over. That is my mission, and those who are not with me in that mission really work against me.

"Blasphemies can be forgiven, except against the Holy Spirit of God; in that blasphemy you equate the Holy Spirit and Satan. If a tree is judged by its fruit, how can anything be expected of you, you collection of vipers? Your own words will condemn you."

Authorities in general aren't used to being talked to in this way, and these particular authorities now decided to challenge Jesus' presumed right to indulge in such impertinence. "Give us a sign," they demanded. "Give us evidence that your claims are legitimate."

"No further evidence will be given to this wicked generation," he replied, "except that of Jonah. Just as Jonah emerged after three days in the belly of a whale, so will the Son of man emerge after three days in the depths of the earth. Those who listened to Jonah will condemn this generation because someone greater than Jonah stands here before it. So will the queen of the South, who traveled so far to hear the words of Solomon, because someone greater than Solomon is here.

"When a demon has left a person and is wandering restlessly about, it may decide to return. If it finds its old home empty, bereft of the Holy Spirit, it will collect some fellow demons to join it in a repossession, and the victim will be worse off than ever. So will it be with this generation."

As he was speaking, his mother and some other relatives arrived and stood outside the house, at the edge of the closely packed crowd. Word of their arrival and of their wish to speak to him was passed along to him. Instead of dropping everything and shoving his way out to them, he took the opportunity to make an observation.

"Who is my mother?" he asked rhetorically. "Who are my brethren?" Then, with a sweeping gesture to his audience he said, "Here they are—all of you who hear the word of God and obey it."

The report we have of this incident is brief and sketchy. It doesn't tell us everything that happened, but just enough to make the point that the bonds of blood are insignificant compared to those of faith and love and were much too weak to distract Jesus from his mission. We have no reason to think that Jesus, after the crowd had dispersed, followed up his remark with a *personal* rejection of his family. At the same time, we do have reason to think that the members of his family were by no means among his most ardent supporters. They seem to have considered him rather odd, at best.

The Parables

A few days later, while preaching on the lakeshore, Jesus presented his audience with a parable drawn, like most of his parables to come, from the land and the ordinary people he knew best.

"A farmer was sowing seed," he said. "Some of the seeds fell near the road and were either trampled underfoot by travelers or were picked up and eaten by birds. Others fell on a thin layer of soil which lightly covered solid rock; with the rock warmed by the sun, they sprouted quickly, but they just as quickly died because they had no proper roots. Others fell in a thicket of brambles which stifled them. But some fell on fertile ground and eventually yielded a rich harvest."

Afterwards some of his disciples asked him if the story had some special meaning and why he used parables in his preaching. "Yes, it has a meaning," he replied, and he was disappointed that they couldn't see it; if *they* didn't understand him, what could be expected of others?

"The seed being sown is my message," he went on to explain. "Some people hear it with no effort to understand it and quickly bury it in corruption or lose it altogether. Others receive it warmly but are too shallow to nurture it within them, and it cannot survive temptation. Still others accept it, but it is stifled under the distractions of this world. Yet it also reaches those who cherish it and patiently nourish it, and they will produce the harvest of faith and love. A rich harvest requires a fertile soil."

"As for parables generally," he continued with more than a touch of wistful irony, "you may not need them because you already have such a firm grasp of the mysteries of the kingdom of heaven. But for others who hear my message without understanding it, parables can be helpful. Those who nourish my message in thoughtful contemplation will be rewarded with greater understanding; those who neglect it will lose it entirely. The greater your effort, the greater your insight will be.

"What is the kingdom of God? How can I even begin to describe it to you except to compare it, in parables, to things you are familiar with? For instance, it is like the story of the farmer who sowed his field with good seed only to find one morning, when the blades began to appear, that someone, under cover of night, had sown weeds in with the wheat. When his hired hands asked if they should pull out the weeds, he told them to wait until harvesttime, when the reapers could pull them out more easily without disturbing the wheat. Then the weeds could be burned and the wheat stored in the barns."

Again he had to explain: the wheat is good, the weeds are evil, and thus will good and evil exist together but be separated and judged at the end of the world.

Jesus used parables often in his efforts to describe the kingdom, and several were collected and brought together in the Gospels. The kingdom, for instance, is like a mustard seed, the tiniest of seeds, which nevertheless grows into a veritable tree. Or like a pinch of yeast spreading throughout a large batch of dough and raising it. Or like a treasure hidden in a field, for which a man will sell all he owns to buy that field. Or like a pearl of great price for which a merchant will give all that he has. Or like a net cast into the sea that brings up all kinds of fish, so that from it the good fish must be chosen and kept and the bad fish thrown away—as it will be at the end of the world when the good and the evil will be separated and the evil will be cast into the furnace amid much weeping and frustrated grinding of teeth.

"Have you understood all this?" Jesus once asked his disciples. Astonishingly, they replied that they had. "Very well," he concluded. "A teacher trained for the kingdom of heaven has a storehouse of things to offer, both old and new."

"Our Name Is Legion"

Later that afternoon Jesus, worn out with preaching, left his audience of the moment on the lakeshore as he and some of his friends, in a few small fishing boats, set out for the eastern shore. Thoroughly exhausted, he immediately went to the stern of the boat and, with his head propped on a cushion, fell fast asleep. On the way across, a storm suddenly arose (the lake was known for such quick changes). The winds whined viciously, whipping the water to a boil while the waves tossed the helpless boats about like corks. But through all the commotion the fatigued Jesus continued sound asleep, even as the boats began to fill. Finally his frightened companions managed to jostle him awake, crying, "We're going under! Don't you care? Don't you care?"

Jesus sat up, stared severely at the surging sea and commanded, "Be quiet!" Submissively, the winds died down; the water grew calm. His friends knew well enough that storms on this lake could subside as quickly as they arose, but this was uncanny. "Who can this be," they murmured incredulously among themselves, "that even the elements obey him?"

They landed not far from a cemetery, a group of hillside caves used as tombs. As they walked by, a large, thoroughly disheveled man, naked and dirty, rushed out toward them. His staggering gait as he ran, his wildly flailing arms, his whole demeanor suggested a raving lunatic. On his wrists and ankles were the remains of fetters; obviously he had been bound with chains which he had broken. He had lived among the tombs for some time now, Jesus and his friends were to learn later, and no one had been able to subdue him. The people of his village considered him hopelessly possessed by demons, and their ostracizing him had done nothing to improve his condition.

Dangerous as he looked, he did Jesus and his friends no harm. Throwing himself on the ground in front of Jesus, he screamed, "Let me be, O Son of God! In God's name, don't torment me!"

A tenet in the lore of Jewish exorcism was that knowing the name of a demon could give one power over it. In this instance Jesus, observing the amenities, asked for the name.

"Our name is Legion," cried the lunatic, who evidently was not above offering a pun even in his rather distraught condition, "because there are so many of us. But please, we beg you, don't send us into the abyss. Send us rather into the swine on the cliffside."

Another tenet: demons could be exorcised from humans and sent into animals, especially "unclean" animals. Jesus glanced above him, and, sure enough, there at the edge of the cliff was a large herd of swine and a herdsman staring down at the noisy scene below him.

Jesus raised his arm, pointing at the swine. "Go into them, then!" he commanded. The lunatic went into convulsions and then lay still, but the swine grew suddenly agitated and began milling around until, with a rush, they all turned toward the cliff and hurled themselves down it, like the legendary lemmings, and fell crashing into the water. The herdsman, after a moment of stupor, disappeared in the direction of the nearest village.

By the time he returned with a crowd of his fellow villagers, the lunatic, clean now and properly clothed, was sitting beside Jesus with a newfound equanimity. They spoke with him, finding his responses perfectly rational; he was quite lucid, in fact. They stared at him and then at Jesus with astonishment and not a little awe. Indeed, their awe quickly sharpened into fright, and soon they were beseeching Jesus to leave the neighborhood immediately. "Curing lunatics is all very well," they seemed to be saying, "but we'd like to hold on to the rest of our swine."

The Daughter of Jairus

Having found no peace and quiet on the eastern shore, Jesus and his companions returned to their boats and recrossed the lake to the western shore, landing at what should have been a relatively deserted spot not far from Capernaum. Evidently they had been seen from the Galilean side long before they arrived, however, for a crowd was already gathering to meet them. In the crowd was a man by the name of Jairus, a leader of the synagogue in Capernaum. After Jesus and his friends had landed and beached the boats, he was among the first to approach them.

Falling at Jesus' feet in a startling show of respect, he begged mercy for his twelve-year-old daughter, who lay close to death at his home in Capernaum. "Come and lay your hands upon her," he entreated Jesus, "so that she may live and be well again."

Jesus nodded compassionately, and the two men headed for the town, with the accompanying crowd buzzing about them like a swarm of bees. As they walked along the road, a woman in the crowd managed to work her way to Jesus' side and to touch his cloak. Jesus started and asked his friends who were nearest to him, "Who touched me?"

His friends looked about them in surprise, relaying the question among themselves and all shaking their heads, almost guiltily. "None of us did," they replied solemnly.

"Someone touched me," Jesus insisted. "I felt power go out of me."

They gestured at the crowd. "In a crushing throng like this, how can you say, 'who touched me'?" They seemed to be asking, almost sardonically, "Who has *not* touched you?"

At this point, fortunately, the woman again made her way to Jesus, this time to offer a diffident explanation. For a dozen years she had been afflicted with a chronic uterine hemorrhage. She had spent all her savings on doctors, to no avail. Since she was considered ritually unclean, she had been afraid to ask anything of Jesus directly but had hoped, confidently, that she would be healed if she could merely touch his cloak. This she had done. Immediately the blood had stopped flowing and she had felt well again. She explained this now very timorously, as though expecting a rebuke for her rash impertinence.

She obviously didn't know Jesus very well. "Daughter," he said to her with a sympathetic smile, "you can be happy, for your faith has healed you. Go in peace."

By now they had arrived at Jairus' house, but before they could enter, a man came out to them with sad news. "Your daughter is dead," he said to Jairus. "There is no need to trouble this rabbi any further."

"No, no," Jesus countered, addressing the stricken Jairus. "Have no fear. Instead, have faith, and she will be healed."

As they entered the house, Jesus could see that the deathbed ceremonies had already begun, with much weeping and loud wailing, as was the custom. "Do not weep," he called to the mourners over the hubbub. "She isn't dead but is only in a coma." Although laughter was hardly an appropriate response under the circumstances, some of the mourners could not suppress some loud snickers at such a seemingly idiotic remark.

Jesus gestured for them to leave, and, with some encouragement from Jairus, they all did. Only Jesus, Jairus and his wife, and three of the disciples remained. Stepping to the bed, Jesus gently took the young girl's hand. She opened her eyes, looked about her, smiled at her mother and father, and sat up. Jairus and his wife stared at her in amazement.

"She should be given something to eat," Jesus suggested matter-of-factly, adding, "Please don't tell anyone about this."

Such minor precautions really were futile, for Jesus could not abandon his mission. The blind continued to be given back their sight, the dumb continued to be given back their voices, and the people continued to have the Good News preached to them. And the uneasy authorities knew perfectly well what he was up to. Mischief, that's what—subversive mischief.

Advice to the Twelve

It was about this time that Jesus decided to begin sending out missionaries. The crowds were so large, and the people seemed so eager for his message, that he needed to spread the workload in order to spread the Word. He also needed to provide some training for those who would carry his message after his death.

And so, one evening after the crowds had dispersed, he gathered together his twelve apostles and explained that he would now be sending them, and perhaps some other disciples, out in pairs to preach the Good News and to heal the sick as he had been doing. For the time being, he advised them, they should confine their activities to within Israel: "Tell the people that the kingdom of God is at hand."

"Travel light," he continued. "Take no extra food, no extra clothes, no extra money. You will be working, and a worker deserves support. When you go into a town or village, find a respectable household that will take you in; stay there, and bring it your peace. If you are refused, shake the dust of that town from your feet and leave. It will see its reckoning on Judgment Day.

"I am sending you out like sheep among wolves, so be as alert as serpents yet as harmless as doves. Don't court disaster; beware of those who would hand you over to courts and synagogues, to governors and kings, for judgment and the whip. Yet when you must testify for me, don't worry over what to say, because the Holy Spirit will give you the words you need.

"My message will turn brother against brother, father against child, children against parents, even to the point of killing. You will, indeed, be persecuted merely for bearing my name. But to those who hold out, patient endurance will bring salvation.

"The servant is not less vulnerable than the master. If the master is called a devil, what worse things may the servant be called! But gather up your courage, for the truth must be made known; what I have told you in whispers, you must proclaim from the housetops.

"Have no fear of those who can kill the body but not the soul.

Rather, fear them who can send both body and soul to perdition. A sparrow, which sells two for a penny in the marketplace, can't fall to the ground without the Father's consent, and you are worth far more to him than many sparrows. Not a hair of your head shall perish. Acknowledge me before the world, and I will acknowledge you before my Father. Only those who deny me before the world will I deny before my Father.

"As I have said, my message will bring not peace but the sword, cleaving families in two. To be worthy of me, one must love me more than father or mother, or son or daughter, and must accept the burden of a cross to follow me. Whoever holds dearly to this life must nonetheless eventually lose it, but whoever gives up this life for my message will receive life in the end.

"Whoever accepts you, accepts me; and whoever accepts me, accepts the Father. And whoever gives merely a cup of water to the humblest person in honor of my message will not, I assure you, go unrewarded."

The Death of the Baptist

Meanwhile a gruesome event had taken place at the lakeshore town of Tiberias, in the palace of Herod Antipas.

Herod was wrestling with a dilemma. He had a grudging respect for the imprisoned Baptist, feared him as a prophet, and irrationally dreaded that his execution might bring on a serious revolt. Yet he also feared (as reported by the historian Josephus) that leaving John alive might permit his following and influence to grow, leading to a worse revolt later on. Further, he was continually badgered by his shrewish wife Herodias to rid the world of the man who had declared their marriage immoral.

Herod was still mulling over the problem when his birthday arrived, forcing him to make a decision quite inadvertently. At an elaborate party, Salome, the daughter of Herodias and evidently a young woman of engrossing talents, put on a dance for Herod and his guests that practically drove him out of his mind. When it was over, he indulged in a grandiloquent display of offering her anything she wanted—even half his kingdom, although it was not really a kingdom and Rome would have instantly overruled any such generosity. She excused herself to consult dutifully with her mother, returning shortly with a prompted request for "John's head on a platter."

Herod couldn't back down without losing face, a face which, in this case, must have been turning several colors. Despite his chagrin, he ordered that the girl's (and her mother's) wish be granted.

Some of John's disciples, on hearing the news, came to the palace, were given the headless corpse, and sadly buried it. Then they left to find Jesus and tell him.

Forebodings 4

The Loaves and Fishes

The news of John's death gave Jesus something to think about. It was a personal loss, of course, but, in addition, it had an ominous ring to it. Herod's anxious preoccupation with John could now be shifted to Jesus, who would hardly welcome such attention. Indeed, John's disciples brought him rumors that the superstitious Herod was already concerned that Jesus, as John's successor, was infused with his spirit. And so, on hearing the news, Jesus withdrew for a while into the countryside to think and pray.

As usual, he soon had company. First his apostles, just returned from their preliminary mission, arrived to report how things had gone. (Apparently they had gone well, all things considered.) Then other disciples began arriving, and then others less committed, until Jesus found himself surrounded by a crowd of several thousand people. As usual also, out of his infinite compassion, he healed their sick and comforted them with news of the kingdom of God.

As the day wore on, some of his more practical disciples pointed out that the people were getting hungry. Jesus stared at them in mock surprise, as though such a possibility had never occurred to him. "Very well," he responded casually, "then give them something to eat."

"Impossible," they protested, "out here in the country." The people should be dismissed so that they could find food in the nearest towns. The only alternative would be for some of the disciples to go into town and buy a king's ransom's worth of food to bring back. But of course they had nothing even approaching a king's ransom.

"Do you have any food at all?" asked Jesus.

"No," one of them replied, "except what a lad has here, but it's only five loaves of barley bread and a couple of fish. Hardly enough to feed *this* crowd."

"That will do," Jesus countered, as solemnly as he could. "Please bring them here."

This they did, though presumably with some muttering about futile gestures. In addition, Jesus asked the apostles to place their traveling baskets on the ground about him. (Jews, when traveling, ordinarily carried some properly prepared food with them in small baskets. Apparently the apostles had finished up their food on the road but were still carrying the empty baskets.) After this was done, Jesus glanced upward for a moment as though to his Father, crumbled the bread and some of the pickled fish into small fragments, and put a bit of both into each of the baskets. "And now," he told his puzzled friends, "have the people sit on the grass, and you can distribute the food."

Reluctantly but obediently, as the crowd settled down, they picked up the baskets and began. To their astonishment, every basket proved to be an inexhaustible cornucopia: as they took food out, it was mysteriously replaced with identical fare. And when everyone had been fed, they still had twelve basketsful left over to take into town for the poor.

Whether they were properly impressed is not recorded, except for a later statement that they were confused. Jesus clearly was trying to tell them something. They had stranger things than this in store for them, and they had to be prepared.

Whatever their reaction, the crowd as a whole was very deeply impressed, but quite improperly. Their murmurs of wonder and appreciation quickly heightened into cries of adulation. "Here indeed is a prophet," went the shouts, "who should be made king of Israel"; these shouts surely found their way back to the authorities. But Jesus would have none of this, of course. After persuading the crowd to disperse, with some help from his friends, he retreated once again, this time to a nearby mountain.

Faith on the Surface

Meanwhile, at his suggestion, some of his friends had gone down to the lakeshore, picked up a boat, and headed for Capernaum where Jesus had arranged to meet them later. The sun had set, and in the dark they soon were bucking a headwind so strong that, even after furling their small sail and resorting to prodigious efforts with the oars, they couldn't be sure whether they were going forward or backward or simply holding their own. Then the wind, not satisfied with merely impeding their progress, became much nastier, churning the sea with such mischievous energy that the boat began to take in water at an alarming rate. They worked away, bailing and rowing, rowing and bailing, for several endless hours. By about four o'clock in the morning, with the storm still in full vigor, they were utterly exhausted.

Then one of them called out and pointed through the gloom to a figure that looked like Jesus coming toward them. Although they all could see him, in their weakened condition they assumed that it was a diabolical apparition of some sort, bent on doing them no good whatsoever. Two or three of them began moaning loudly in terror.

But Jesus' voice came to them across the water and through the wind, "Take heart. It is I. Don't be afraid."

Peter, who was in the group of hapless sailors, impulsively answered, "If it's really you, Lord, let me come to you on the water."

"Come on, then," replied Jesus, and Peter, after scrambling out of the boat, began walking confidently toward him. The wind proved too intimidating, however; losing his confidence, he began to sink. "Lord," he cried out in panic, "save me!"

Jesus held out his hand, pulled him up, and walked with him to the boat as the wind began to grow quiet. "O you man of little faith," he said to Peter in a tone of disappointment, "why did you give in to doubt?" While Peter mumbled in embarrassment, they got into the boat. The others, numb with fatigue and amazement, unfurled the sail like so many automatons and set a course for the distant shore.

How Jesus happened to show up so fortuitously we don't know. A curious remark in the Gospel of Mark, to the effect that he almost passed them by, suggests that he had simply decided to take this as the shortest, simplest route (for someone with his talents) regardless of the weather and was unaware of his friends' plight until he heard their calls of distress. This seems unlikely; it is not suggested in either of the other accounts of the incident. Yet we know so little about what Jesus knew, and how he knew it, that anything seems possible.

The Bread of Life

The next morning, when the free-meal crowd discovered that Jesus had taken French leave during the night, they remembered that his disciples had set out for the vicinity of Capernaum in the evening, and a large number of them hurried off in that direction.

Jesus had already arrived in town and was at the synagogue when they finally caught up with him. "When did you get here?" some of them asked.

Ignoring the pointless question, Jesus gave them a searching look. He recognized many of them and wanted to be friendly, but he had no intention of becoming a permanently renewable meal ticket. "You have come looking for me," he accused them, "because yesterday you ate so heartily. You'd do better to worry, not about such perishable food, but rather about the food of eternal life that the Son of man will give you with the blessing of God the Father."

Apparently they caught his drift, vaguely, and decided to humor him: "What must we do to carry out God's work?"

"What God requires," answered Jesus, "is that you believe in his messenger."

This gave them an opening, an opportunity to inveigle him into doing that food trick again: "What proof can you give for such a claim, so that we may see it and believe you? What can you do? Our ancestors ate manna in the wilderness. As the Scriptures say, 'He gave them bread from heaven to eat.'"

Jesus refused to rise to the bait. "I assure you," he responded, "that it wasn't Moses; it was my Father who provided that bread from heaven. The bread that comes from heaven is the bread of God which gives life to the world."

This comment provided another opening. Their reaction was like that of the Samaritan woman at Jacob's well. "Then, sir, from now on furnish us with this bread." By now, presumably, saliva glands were operating at full flow.

But Jesus was no less determined than they. "I am that bread of life," he persisted. "Whoever believes in me will know neither hunger nor thirst. But you, though you have seen me and what I have done, you don't really believe in me.

"I will reject no one who comes to me as a trust from my Father, for I have come here from heaven to do his will, not mine. It is his will that all who see the Son and believe in him shall be raised up by me at the end of this world and shall live forever."

His audience had begun muttering as soon as he had identified himself with the bread from heaven. He had parried their demands, and their frustration began turning into resentment. "Isn't this Jesus, the son of Joseph?" they grumbled among themselves. "Don't we know his father and mother? How can he say that he has come down out of heaven?"

"Stop your murmuring," Jesus adjured them. "No one can come

to me to be raised up on the last day except from the Father. The prophets have said that all will be informed by God. Those who accept the truth from the Father will come to me. They have not seen the Father—only his messenger has seen him—but whoever believes will live forever. I *am* the bread of life. Your ancestors ate the manna in the wilderness, but eventually they died. I am the living bread from heaven, and whoever eats this bread will live eternally."

He stopped speaking. The muttering had died down, and his audience stared at him in silence. He wanted their full attention since he had something shocking to say.

"Indeed," he continued, almost defiantly, "the bread that I speak of is my flesh offered for the life of the world."

After a moment of stunned speechlessness, the crowd erupted in cries of disbelief. "How can this man give us his flesh to eat?!" The reaction was enough to deter a weaker man, but Jesus, far from withdrawing or softening his provocative assertion, went on to emphasize it and even to elaborate on it.

"I'm telling you the truth," he insisted. "Unless you eat the flesh of the Son of man and drink his blood"—here there were many sharp intakes of breath, for the drinking of blood would be especially abominable to Jews—"you have no life in you. Those who eat my flesh and drink my blood have everlasting life, and I will raise them up on the last day; for my flesh is truly food, and my blood is truly drink. Those who eat my flesh and drink my blood are in union with me, and I with them. Just as the living Father has made me his messenger, just as I live because of him, so whoever eats me will live because of me. *This* is the bread from heaven, and whoever eats it will, unlike your ancestors, live forever."

By now the synagogue was ringing with tumultuous controversy. Jesus became aware that many of his own disciples were exclaiming, "This is hard to accept. Who can even listen to it?"

"Is this a stumbling block for you?" he asked them. "But suppose you were to see the Son of man ascending to where he came from, what then? It is the spirit that gives life; the flesh itself means nothing. The words I have spoken to you are spirit and bring life." Then with a sigh he said, "Still, some of you won't believe me. This is why I said that whoever comes to me will have accepted the truth from the Father."

He was right. Many of his disciples deserted him as of that moment, returning to their former lives and occupations. As they began leaving, he gathered his apostles together and asked whether they, too, would leave him.

Peter answered for them. "To whom else could we turn?" he asked rhetorically. "You have the words of eternal life, and we know that you are God's holy one."

Jesus was touched; yet his answer was a curious one. "To think that I chose you twelve," he exclaimed as though preoccupied with a sudden, unwelcome thought, "and yet one of you is a devil!"

As for the free-meal crowd, they quickly dispersed. He had given them more food than they had bargained for, but it was food for thought. And as for the free meal, they weren't hungry any longer.

On Cleanliness and Godliness

A day or so later, as Jesus was preaching, some authorities from Jerusalem showed up and joined the crowd. At the first opportunity, one of them broke in with a prepared question clearly designed for heckling, "Why do your disciples consistently disregard the official rules about washing one's hands before a meal?"

This was one of the countless ceremonial rules imposed by the authorities on the hapless people to keep not only the hands but also cups, jars, pots, pans, and other paraphernalia free from possible foreign contamination. Among ordinary people, who had less leisure time than the authorities for ritual niceties, it apparently was a rule more honored in breach than in observance. But its neglect offered the authorities an opportunity for imperious disapproval and bureaucratic meddling.

Jesus, as was his wont in dealing with these shriveled minds, declined to offer anything resembling a respectful explanation, but rather launched a counterattack. For ammunition he brought up "Corban," the surrender of property or income to God—or, more immediately, to the priests, who had conveniently ruled that it took precedence over other obligations, including the duty to provide for one's aged parents.

"Why," he challenged the needlers, "do you hold so fast to human regulations at the expense of God's commandments? God told us, through Moses, to honor father and mother, yet you will not allow anyone under the pledge of Corban to do anything to help them. And this is only a sample of the sort of thing you do habitually. Isaiah, indeed, spoke for God when he said of you hypocrites,

'These people honor me with their lips,
    but their hearts are far from me.
They worship me in vain,
    offering human rules as doctrine.'

"Listen, and try to understand," he concluded, addressing the crowd in general. "Nothing from outside can enter and defile a person. What can defile a person comes from inside."

This pretty well undermined the authorities' ceaseless warnings against contamination. Once again he had defeated them with their own weapons. Afterwards, several of Jesus' friends expressed some alarm. "Did you notice," they asked him, "how deeply offended the authorities were by that remark?"

"Yes," he nodded, "but every plant not put there by my Father must be pulled up. Don't worry about those people. They are blind leaders. If the blind lead the blind, all will fall into the ditch."

"Then please explain the remark," asked Peter.

"You still don't understand? Don't you see that what goes into the body simply goes through it and then out as harmless waste? But out from the heart come wicked intentions, murders, adultery, thievery, lies, violent anger, and other evil things."

Presumably Peter nodded, but rather numbly. This wasn't the sort of thing that he had heard stressed in synagogue. The novelty would have to wear off before the message could sink in.

"Who Do You Say I Am?"

Again in need of a little peace and quiet, Jesus and his friends left Galilee and spent the next few days in the Phoenician country to the north. Apparently they did find some rest there, for the account of their visit records only a single incident.

They had taken lodgings in a house without attracting attention, but toward the end of their stay a woman appeared and asked for help. She had just come from her home, where her daughter lay grievously ill—possessed by a demon, she said. Jesus' friends at first tried to protect him from her, but she became so persistent in her entreaties that they finally asked him to do something, if only to get rid of her before the whole neighborhood descended on them.

He agreed, and they brought her to him. Since she was a Gentile, he may have decided to use the occasion to make a point for the benefit of his disciples. After she had greeted him—flatteringly as the "Son of David"—and had told him her story, he remained silent for a long moment and then replied coldly, much as an orthodox Jew might be expected to treat a heathen. "The children of Israel must first be satisfied," he said. "It wouldn't be right to give the children's bread to the dogs." ("The dogs" was a not uncommon term for Gentiles in the Jewish authorities' lexicon of xenophobia.)

Doubtless Jesus sensed that this woman was not the sort who would simply turn away crestfallen. On the contrary, she had an answer for him and a rather clever one at that. "But, sir," she protested, "even dogs snatch up the crumbs that drop from the children's table!"

Jesus smiled in appreciation. "For such a reply, and for your faith," he said, "the demon has left your daughter. Go home and see."

She left, accompanied by a couple of the disciples. They found the girl lying quietly in her bed, exhausted but on her way to recovery.

This, however, was no way to foster continued peace and quiet. To avoid the commotion that news of the cure was sure to cause, Jesus and company headed back to Galilee. Once there, they stopped to rest on a mountainside not far from town. But soon their rest was interrupted.

The first group to reach Jesus included a man who was deaf and also suffered from a speech impediment. The others, speaking for him, begged that he be cured. Curiously, Jesus in response followed a formula traditionally used in faith healing, perhaps to show his disciples its irrelevance, since he seldom went through such motions. He touched the man's ears, put a bit of his own saliva on the man's tongue, looked up to heaven, and said, "Be opened!" The man's friends crowded about him and spoke to him. He heard them and replied, quite articulately.

In the ensuing excitement Jesus tried to ask them not to publicize the incident, but he might just as well have asked the surrounding shrubs. It isn't only the deaf who don't hear. Before long he and his companions were surrounded by a tumultuous crowd, eagerly presenting relatives and friends to be cured—as the Gospel of Matthew puts it, "the lame, the maimed, the blind, the dumb, and many others." As usual, Jesus could not refuse them.

As the news of the healing spread, people came from an ever-widening circle, until the crowd numbered several thousand. Both accounts of this episode also report that it lasted three days (whatever that may mean), but presumably the crowd fluctuated in number and makeup with continual arrivals and departures. At any rate, Jesus and his companions were once again confronted with the problem of feeding their hungry guests in the barren countryside, the food supply on this occasion consisting of seven barley loaves and "a few small fish." And so again Jesus resorted to on-the-spot multiplication: the food was distributed, all were fed, and seven basketsful were left over.

That evening the crowd thinned out enough to permit Jesus and company to make their way to the lakeshore and take a boat, or boats, to a point on the shore a little farther north. Soon after landing, they were accosted by a passel of disputatious authorities. As the others had done earlier, they demanded "a sign from heaven" as proof of Jesus' claims.

"When the sky is red in the evening," Jesus replied stoically, referring to a characteristic of the Palestinian climate, "you say that tomorrow the weather will be fair. And when the sky is threatening in the morning, you say that today the weather will be foul. You can read the skies, but you can't see the signs of the times all about you. Well, you can expect no such sign as you ask for, but only the sign of Jonah." Turning on his heel, he left them, followed by his friends.

As they proceeded along the road to Bethsaida, his friends grew hungry, and this reminded them that they had forgotten to bring along any food. So when Jesus, in the course of their conversation, warned them to "beware of the leaven of the Pharisees and Sadducees," they assumed that he thought they had taken some bread from the well-stocked authorities during their recent encounter.

"But we didn't take any bread," one of them protested.

"O you men of little faith," Jesus complained, sensing their problem, "why do you devote so much thought to the lack of bread? Didn't you notice, or can't you recall, the thousands of people who were fed with five loaves, or the other thousands who were fed with seven? Don't you really know that I wasn't talking about bread? Do you still not understand?"

After some cooperative cudgeling, and despite their hunger, they did begin to understand. This was another metaphor. They should beware of the teaching of the authorities. Bread really didn't enter into it.

As they entered Bethsaida, a blind man was brought to them for healing. This story has an odd literary touch, although it is told only in the rather artless and straightforward Gospel of Mark. Jesus took the man by the hand and led him out of town to a less conspicuous location. He touched the man's eyes with a bit of saliva and then asked him, "Can you see anything?"

After opening his eyes and peering about for a moment, the man answered, "Yes, I see people, I think, but they look like trees walking about." Since this was hardly ideal, Jesus touched his eyes again, and the trees became people, unmistakably. Finally Jesus asked the excited man and his excited friends, who evidently were farmers, to go directly home without going into town. It was a small request, and perhaps they granted it, for the brief visit to the town by Jesus and his companions seems to have been relatively uneventful.

Soon Jesus and his friends were on their way north again, to visit the country centered on Caesarea Philippi and near Mount Hermon, then, as now, the source of the Jordan River. On the way they fell into a discussion of Jesus' reputation.

"Who do people say I am?" Jesus asked at one point.

Their answers varied: John the Baptist, Elijah, Jeremiah, or another of the prophets.

"And how about you?" Jesus continued. "Who do you say I am?"

"You are the Christ, the Messiah," quickly answered Peter the impulsive, "the Son of the living God."

"You are especially blessed," responded Jesus, "because this was revealed to you by none other than my Father in heaven. Indeed, you are Peter, the rock on which I will build my church, that the forces of evil may not prevail against it. I will give you the keys of the kingdom: what you enjoin on earth will be enjoined in heaven, and what you allow on earth will be allowed in heaven."

There is no record of Peter's reaction, possibly because he was too stunned to have any visible reaction. In fact, the record of this conversation ends abruptly, with Jesus warning his disciples to tell no one about his being the Messiah. The title, with its strong political overtones, could too readily mislead the eagerly expectant people and antagonize the anxiously expectant authorities.

Suffering and Glory

The authorities' anxiety was a source of anxiety to Jesus. He seems to have had a clear picture of his ultimate fate, or at least of its essentials; he seems also to have worried over whether it would occur prematurely, before he could complete his mission, however closely that fate and that mission may have been intertwined. In connection with his warning to his disciples to be quiet about his being the Messiah, he tried to make it clear that he wasn't merely being coy.

He was destined to go to Jerusalem, he explained, and suffer much pain and humiliation at the hands of the priests and other authorities. He would be executed but would return from the grave three days later. The Gospel of Mark states that he made this quite plain, although the disciples' later conduct suggests that he didn't make it plain enough.

Peter's immediate reaction to this information was to reproach him for painting so gloomy a picture and to deny the prediction quite flatly, "No, sir, this could never happen to you." But Jesus, for whom the prospect was fearful enough without further discouragement from his friends, in turn rebuked him with an unusual harshness: "Away with you, Satan! You are wrapped up in human concerns, not God's."

"If anyone wishes to follow me," he continued, not only to Peter but also generally to the disciples and some others who had joined them, "let him forsake his own interests and shoulder his cross each day. Whoever is concerned with preserving this life will lose it anyway, but whoever loses it for my sake will find life instead. How does it benefit anyone to win the world and lose one's soul? Is anything worth trading for one's soul?

"If anyone is ashamed of me and my message, so will the Son of man be ashamed of that person when he comes in glory to render his judgments. And I tell you, some of you here will live to see the kingdom of God established."

About a week later Jesus evidently decided to give his three principal disciples a sample of the "glory" that he had been talking about. Taking Peter and the two brothers James and John up onto a mountain (Mount Hermon, according to one tradition), he left them for a moment and went on a short distance by himself to pray. While he was praying, their attention was attracted by a bright light. Looking in his direction, they could see him in a transfigured state; his face was shining brilliantly, his clothes were a dazzling white. Within the radiance two men appeared, the prophet Elijah and Moses, talking with him; the disciples could make out that they were discussing his coming death and achievement of his mission in Jerusalem.

Peter's curious reaction was more that of a carpenter than a fisherman. "Lord, it's good we're here," he called. "Let us set up three memorials on that spot, one each for you and Elijah and Moses!"

At that moment, quite fortuitously, he and the others became conscious of a cloud enveloping them and a voice within it saying, "This is my beloved Son. Listen to him." As they stood there gaping, the cloud slowly dissipated, and they found Jesus standing there with them in reassuringly familiar form. Since his first words were a warning to tell no one of this experience, Peter dropped his suggestion about the memorials. As the Gospel of Luke puts it, he hadn't realized what he was saying.

Actually, Jesus' warning contained a modifying clause, and on their way down the mountainside he emphasized it. "Tell no one of what you've seen," he cautioned them, "until the Son of man has risen from the dead." The disciples were puzzled; the notion of the Messiah's death was harder for them to accept, both intellectually and emotionally, than that of his resurrection.

Grasping at a straw of hope, one of them argued, "But the authorities say that Elijah must come first." They were implying rather wistfully that all this talk of death could be premature.

Jesus quickly disillusioned him, however. "Yes," he replied, "but Elijah has already come. They failed to recognize him and treated him just as they wished, much as they will treat the Son of man." And it dawned on them that he was speaking of John the Baptist.

At the foot of the mountain they were met by a large crowd. From it a man ran up to Jesus and begged for help: "Rabbi, have mercy on my son, if you can. He suffers greatly from epilepsy. His fits throw him about and injure him, and have even hurled him into a fire and into dangerous waters. I asked your disciples to cure him, but they couldn't do it."

"O you people of little faith," exclaimed Jesus with a dismayed glance at his disciples, "how long must I put up with you? And you"— turning to the distressed father—"did you say, 'if you can'? To whoever has faith, anything is possible."

The father's answer was cunning, though doubtless sincere: "Then, sir, cure my disbelief!" Jesus evidently found this request irresistible, for both father and son were cured.

Later the disciples asked him why they hadn't been able to cure the boy. "Because of your little faith," he replied. "I tell you, if you have genuine faith, though it be as small as a mustard seed, you can say to this mountain, 'Move!' and it will move. Nothing will be impossible for you."

On their return to Galilee the disciples were still marveling at some of the wonders he had performed on their most recent travels, but he cautioned them again that their faith was to be sorely tried. "Let my warning sink in," he admonished them. "The Son of man will be given over to human justice and executed, to rise after three days." But they found this too depressing to accept, especially since they didn't really understand it.

Threat and Defiance 5

Their arrival in Capernaum was rather badly timed; it was the day for payment of the annual temple tax, and the tax collectors had strategically set up their booths at various unavoidable locations within the town. The tax amounted to half a shekel, a shekel being about what a fisherman would get for a large catch. As Jesus and company passed by one of the booths, a tax collector caught Peter by the cloaktail and asked severely, "Doesn't your rabbi pay the tax?" Peter, perhaps feeling that this wasn't his responsibility, answered with a laconic "yes" and pulled away.

Jesus evidently had overheard this exchange, however, and when they arrived at his house, he called Peter to him. "What do you think?" he asked. "Do the kings of this world demand tribute from their own sons, or from others?"

"Why, from others," replied Peter.

"Then a son is exempt," smiled Jesus, suggesting that a tax paid to God should not be collected from his Son. "However, we mustn't offend them; so go down to the lake and throw out a line. If you open the mouth of the first fish you catch, you'll find a shekel in it. Take it and pay the tax for you and me." Peter did as he was told, presumably without seeing any humor in the situation at all.

On Humility and Forgiveness

Meanwhile some of the apostles had fallen into a rather heated discussion. When Jesus asked them what they were talking about, they retreated into an embarrassed silence, since they had been arguing over who would rank highest in the kingdom of heaven, which they generally considered to be just around the corner.

Jesus—who had been aware of, if not impressed by, their conversation—called the apostles together for a little straightening out. Signaling a small boy playing just outside to come in, he placed him on his knee and addressed himself to the apostles' concern.

"Whoever wants to rank first will rank last and serve all the others," he told them. "I tell you, unless you forget such ambition and become like little children, you won't even enter the kingdom of heaven. Only those as humble as this boy will be great in that kingdom. Further, those who care for these little ones thereby care for me and for the Father who sent me. And conversely, whoever leads one of them to sin would be better off with a millstone on his neck at the bottom of the sea. Occasions for evil do arise in this world, but woe to those through whom they arise!

"And so beware of despising the humble and lowly; they have angels in heaven representing them to the Father. If a shepherd has a hundred sheep and loses one, won't he leave the ninety-nine to look for the lost one and, indeed, rejoice more over finding the one than over having the ninety-nine? That is the way it will be with your Father over the loss of a little one." After a pause, he turned to a related subject.

"If your brother wrongs you, first take up the matter with him alone. If he denies the wrong, confront him with two or three witnesses. If he refuses to listen to them, report the matter before the congregation. If he remains adamant, he must then be ostracized, treated as the Jews treat Gentiles and tax collectors. Wherever two or three or more congregate in my name, I am there among them."

"But how often should I forgive my brother?" asked Peter doubtfully. "As much as seven times?"

"No, not seven," Jesus replied, "but seventy times seven, and more. This reminds me of the king who wanted to settle an enormous debt owed to him by one of his nobles. When he found that the noble couldn't pay, he commanded that all his property and even his family be sold to raise the money. But the noble begged him for more time, and the king took pity on him and canceled the debt.

"On the way out of the palace the noble met a man who owed him a much smaller amount. Collaring the man, he insisted on immediate repayment. When the man asked for more time, the noble refused and shortly thereafter had him thrown into debtors' prison. Some enraged friends of the man reported this to the king who summoned the noble, explained forgiveness to him, and handed him over to the jailors for payment of the now-reinstated debt. So will my heavenly Father treat you if you fail to forgive your brothers from the bottom of your heart."

At this point the apostle John broke in to report that a man had been discovered exorcising in Jesus' name, but the disciples had stopped him because "he wasn't one of us."

This must have been discouraging for Jesus, considering how strongly he had been condemning the "one of us" attitude on the part of the authorities. "There was no reason to restrain him," he replied. "No one who works wonders in my name is likely, then, to disparage me. Whoever isn't against us is on our side."

A Source of Dissension

When the time arrived for the Feast of Tabernacles, a major festival lasting eight days, Jesus' relatives in Galilee prepared for a pilgrimage to Jerusalem to observe the occasion in proper style. They urged him to join them. When he expressed reluctance, they helpfully informed him that it was stupid for anyone who needed publicity to stay so withdrawn in Galilee, far from the festival crowds. His disciples in Judea deserved to see what he could do; indeed, he should prove himself to the world.

Jesus was by no means insensitive to their sardonic tone. He knew they had little or no faith in him; in fact, they seemed uncertain over whether he was a lunatic or a charlatan. If he joined them, he might win some of them over; but that was not his mission. Further, they would be traveling to Jerusalem in a caravan, very conspicuously. He had reason to think that the authorities in Judea now had designs on his life, and this gave him pause, since he might not get to the city without being picked up and neutralized in one way or another. And so he told his family, as they were about to leave, that it was high time for them to go, but not for him.

He did make the trip, however, three or four days later, alone and inconspicuously. He discovered that the people there were asking about him and discussing him—though almost in whispers for fear the authorities would get wind of their subversive conversations. There was a good deal of argument about him, with some saying that he was a good man and others condemning him for misleading the people.

He may have felt, as a result, that he might be missing a golden opportunity. At any rate, once he was within the temple walls, he began to preach. He was in good form. As a crowd gathered round and listened to him, people began exclaiming over how learned he seemed to be, especially for someone without the conventional academic credentials.

He heard these remarks and replied, "My teaching comes not from me alone, but from him who sent me. Whoever habitually obeys him will know instinctively whether these words are merely mine or his. A teacher who broadcasts his own opinions may be untrustworthy because he seeks his own glory, but a teacher who works for the glory of the one who sent him, that teacher is honorable and tells the truth."

"Moses gave you the Law, didn't he?" he continued, his voice rising a notch. "Yet you don't live up to it. Otherwise, why are there plans to kill me?"

"You're out of your mind!" someone shouted. "Who's planning to kill you?"

Jesus answered the question with an oblique reference to those who objected to his healing on the Sabbath. "With one kind of work I have caused great consternation. Moses commanded the rite of circumcision, and so circumcisions today are performed on the Sabbath as necessary, to avoid breaking a higher law. Yet haven't I been denounced for making a person well on the Sabbath? I ask for judgment in this, not on appearances but on reasonable grounds."

As he continued speaking, murmurs arose in the crowd. "This *is* the man the authorities want to get rid of," some said, "and here he is, speaking without hindrance; maybe they think he really is the Messiah." "No," argued others, "we know where this man came from, but tradition has it that the Messiah will come unexpectedly."

Jesus heard this and answered in a piercing voice, "Yes, you know me and where I'm from. But I'm not here by my own authority; it is the one who sent me that you do not know. Yet I know him because I'm his messenger." When he said this, some of the authorities who had joined the crowd were eager to arrest him, although no one did. As for the people, many were much impressed with him and his reputation. "When the Messiah does come," they wondered among themselves, "what better proofs will he give than this fellow has given?"

This sort of talk quickly reached the sensitive ears of the chief temple authorities, who thereupon sent a squad of temple police to arrest Jesus and bring him to them. But as the squad approached the crowd, Jesus saw them and put them off with a cryptic promise to the people generally, "I'll be here with you only a little while longer, and then I'll return to him who sent me. You'll look for me but won't find me. Where I shall be you cannot come."

Among some of his listeners this aroused a puzzled curiosity. "What does he mean, that we won't find him? Will he visit the Jews who live among the Greeks? Is he going to preach to the Greeks? What is this place, where we can't come?" But Jesus, unwilling to be more specific, faded into the crowd, eluding the bemused police.

A couple of days later, on the last day of the feast, he resurfaced and resumed his preaching, again creating dissension among his listeners. They weren't used to such statements as "Whoever is thirsty can come to me and drink, for those who believe in me will find me a fountain of living water." Some insisted that this man *must* be the Messiah, while others insisted with equal vigor that he couldn't be, since the Messiah was to be a descendant of King David from Bethlehem, and this man was a carpenter from Nazareth. And again some of the authorities present were eager, if unable, to arrest him.

The men able to arrest him, the temple police, let him fade into the crowd again and get away. On their return to the temple officials, their squad leader explained their empty hands by saying, in effect, that Jesus had mesmerized them: "No one has ever said things like that!"

"You mean he has bamboozled you as well?" cried one of the assembled pooh-bahs in disgust. "Has anyone in authority ever believed in him? Of course not! It's only the cursed rabble, who know nothing of the Law!" Presumably the temple police retired diffidently from the scene.

Among the panjandrums present was Nicodemus, Jesus' undercover visitor, whose basic fairness and common sense had survived the pressures of status and associations. "Does our Law condemn a man without hearing what he has to say for himself," he interjected, "and without learning just what he's done?"

The question earned him no Brownie points in that company. "Oh, are you from Galilee, too?" he was asked accusingly. "Go look through the Scriptures, and you'll realize that prophets do not come from Galilee!"

And the meeting adjourned.

"I Am"

The next morning, as he was sitting alone on the broad porch of the temple, Jesus was accosted by some authorities and a couple of policemen with a forlorn-looking woman in tow. Ordering her placed before him, and in front of a small crowd that had begun to gather, their eminences informed him that the woman had been "caught while committing an act of adultery," an act for which, they hastened to remind him, Moses had commanded stoning as a punishment (for women, that is). What, they asked, was his opinion?

Jesus, who was sitting on a stone step low enough for him to reach the ground comfortably, bent over and began idly doodling in the thin layer of sand that covered the pavement. He needed a moment to think. Since he didn't for an instant believe that they were really interested in his opinion, he was sure they were setting a trap. If he advised stoning the woman, perhaps later they could accuse him of inciting others to murder, or at least of rendering a serious judgment without proper authority; if he advised otherwise, perhaps they could accuse him of condoning adultery. He continued doodling until, impatiently savoring their imminent triumph, they began to pester him for an answer.

Finally he raised his head and, looking at them squarely, replied, "Any of you who are free from sin should throw the first stone." No stone was thrown, no word was said in response; so he returned to his doodling.

Gradually the crowd—authorities, police, and people—quietly melted away, with the eldest first to go. Eventually only Jesus and the woebegone woman were left. Jesus looked at her and smiled.

"Where is everybody?" he asked her. "Hasn't anyone condemned you?"

"No, sir," she replied. "No one."

"Well, then, neither do I," he said. "Go on your way, and sin no further."[1]

A little later a cluster of Pharisees and some others caught sight of him as he was passing the temple treasury room; they approached him and asked him just who he considered himself to be.

Jesus was not given to answering such questions in the style of name, rank, and serial number. His identity was a mystical thing, and so was his answer. "I am the light of the world," he replied. "Those who follow me won't walk in the dark but will have the light of life."

"But you are offering testimony in your own behalf," one of the Pharisees objected, amid much nodding in confused agreement. "Such testimony is legally invalid."

Jesus never seemed to be able to take these dignitaries very seriously, however deadly their enmity. In this instance their position was sound enough in logic and law, but he chose to answer them almost playfully, on a level where their footing would be less secure.

[1] This story is told only in the Gospel of John and is omitted in some of the more reliable manuscripts. But it offers so strong a moral and is so much in character that it was not about to be omitted here.

"My testimony is no less true," he said, skirting the legal issue of credibility, "just because it's mine. I know where I'm from and where I'm headed, but you don't. You judge by appearances; I don't. If I do any judging, I do it not on my own but with my Father, whose messenger I am. Under your law the testimony of two people is acceptable, and that's the case here. I testify in my behalf, and so does my Father."

His hecklers looked about them elaborately and asked, "And just where is your father?"

In reply Jesus reduced the whole argument to a final absurdity. "You know neither me nor my Father; indeed, if you knew me, you'd know my Father also." This left them sputtering in some confusion, but it was becoming ever clearer that the only way to shut this fellow up would be to shut him up literally, in jail or in a grave.

In fact, he continued speaking now. "I am going away," he promised again. "Without me, you will die unforgiven, for where I'm going you cannot come." And again his listeners buzzed with curiosity, this time speculating on whether he meant to commit suicide.

"You are creatures of this world," Jesus explained opaquely, "and I am not. And that is why I say you will die unforgiven unless you believe I am he."

"He? Who?" exclaimed several of them. "Who are you, anyway?"

"The one of whom I've told you from the outset," replied Jesus. "I'll have more to say, and what I say will be the truth from the one who sent me. When you have raised the Son of man on high, then you may finally recognize me and my message as coming from the Father."

Some people who had stopped to listen were nodding, as though tentatively accepting his claims, and to these he addressed a similarly tentative promise. "If you keep faith with my message," he assured them, "then you are indeed my disciples. You will know the truth, and the truth will make you free."

"But we are descendants of Abraham," protested one of the authorities, "and have never given ourselves in slavery to anyone. So how can you say we'll be made free?"

"I tell you," Jesus replied, "whoever yields to sin becomes its slave. A slave is not a recognized, permanent member of the family, but a son is. So if the Son sets you free, you will have freedom in truth. I know that you are children of Abraham; yet you are my mortal enemies because my message makes no headway among you. That message is from my Father, but you prefer the counsel of *your* father."

"But Abraham is our father," the Pharisee protested, unaware that Jesus had a much different father in mind.

"If you were truly Abraham's children," answered Jesus, "you would behave as such. But Abraham was never engaged in eliminating a messenger of God. He is not the father whose advice you follow."

"We're not bastards!" protested the spokesman. "Indeed, in the end we all have only one Father, God himself."

"If God were your Father," retorted Jesus, "you would give me your love and trust, because I have come from him and because he appointed me his messenger. But you won't understand my message because you won't listen to it.

"No, you are children of the devil, and you carry out his will. He has been a murderer since the dawn of human life and is the fountainhead of lies. Thus it's because I speak the truth that you won't believe me. Who among you can justly accuse me of sin? If no one, then why not believe me? Children of God would listen to his message. But because you're not, you won't."

"Aren't we correct," asked the bewildered but indignant spokesman, falling back to a defense line of group prejudice, "in saying you are a Samaritan and are possessed?"

Jesus ignored the quasi-racial slur. "No, I'm not possessed," he replied wearily. "I pay honor to the Father while you dishonor me. I seek no glory for myself; someone else will see to that. I simply tell you that whoever stays true to my message will not suffer death in eternity."

"Now we *know* you're possessed!" came the reply. "Abraham is dead, and so are the prophets, yet you claim that whoever stays true to your message will not suffer death. Are you greater than our father Abraham who died, and greater than the prophets who also died? Just who do you make yourself out to be?"

Jesus was getting deeper and deeper now with every word, but he seemed to be choosing the words quite carefully. "Were I to glorify myself," he answered, "such glory would be empty. My glory comes from my Father, whom you call your God. You may not know him, but I do; were I to deny this, I'd be as much of a liar as you all are.

"As for your father Abraham, he rejoiced at my coming; he saw it, and it gladdened him."

"What?" the spokesman snorted. "You, who aren't yet fifty years old, you've seen Abraham?"

"Let me assure you," said Jesus, taking a deep breath, "before Abraham even was born, *I am.*"

After a moment of shocked silence came the deluge of abusive protest. "I Am" was the most sacred of the traditional Hebrew words for the one true God, and here was this upstart flaunting his blasphemy in the very temple of that God. Someone picked up a stone and threw it at him, though it fell short. Then several others picked up stones, but their target faded from their view and could not be found again.

Jesus had fled the temple grounds, for "his time had not yet come." He must live to die another day.

Samaritans, Unfriendly and Otherwise

The record of Jesus' itinerary seems rather muddled at this point, as it is elsewhere. Being a wandering preacher and not a tourist, Jesus was hardly ever likely to say, "If today is Tuesday, this must be Bethany."

After leaving Jerusalem, he seems to have returned to Galilee, but not for very long. He wandered about for some time in Samaria, Perea, and Judea, with occasional visits to Jerusalem. Although that city clearly was his final destination, his approach to it was anything but a straight line.

In one Samaritan town the people, upon learning that he and his companions were headed for the capital city of their religious rivals, refused to receive them. This angered James and John, who suggested destroying the town with fire from heaven, but Jesus rebuked them for such arsonist talk, and they all went on quietly to another village.

Apparently they encountered this sort of inhospitality fairly often, especially in Samaria, so that sometimes they found themselves in the predicament of having no place to stay the night except in the open countryside. On one occasion, when someone eagerly offered to follow him wherever he might go, Jesus warned wryly that doing so could be uncomfortable: "Foxes have holes and birds have nests, but the Son of man has nowhere to lay his head."

Following him, he also said, involved more than a casual decision. To one man who said that he would have to attend his father's funeral before leaving to follow Jesus, he suggested that this be left to other relatives: "Let the dead bury their own dead while you spread the news of the kingdom." Another wanted to return home first to say good-bye, but Jesus replied that a plowman who looks back will plow a crooked furrow: "Whoever puts his hand to the plow and then looks back isn't ready for the kingdom of God." Whatever the exaggeration here, Jesus, in general, can hardly be thought of as inviting halfhearted commitments from his disciples.

The commitment of most of the disciples evidently was wholehearted enough to produce wonders of healing and exorcism for them, or at least so they reported to Jesus on returning from their missionary excursions. Jesus' response to these reports was a mystical one, describing visions in which he had seen the prince of evil falling like "lightning from heaven" as a result of their efforts. However, he cautioned them, rather than exulting in their gift of power over evil, they might better rejoice in the promise that their names were "written in heaven."

In a similarly mystical vein, he had some rejoicing of his own to do, thanking his Father for acquainting simple, humble people with mysteries indiscernible to the learned and sophisticated. He thanked him, too, for his own unique understanding of—and by—the Father, an understanding which he could now at least partly share with others of his choosing. To his disciples he offered private encouragement, assuring them of the high privilege in their current position: "Many prophets and kings wanted to see and hear such things as you have seen and heard, but they neither saw nor heard them."

In contrast, shortly thereafter he had a much more practical discussion with a scribe who asked what he should do to earn eternal life.

"What does the Law have to say?" asked Jesus. "How do you read it?"

"It tells us, love the Lord your God with all your heart and soul, with all your strength and all your mind and love your neighbor as you love yourself."

"Precisely," Jesus replied. "Do that, and you'll have eternal life."

This answer might well have satisfied a sincere questioner, but the scribe had a little argumentative jousting to do. After a moment of probing for a weak spot, he asked, "And just who is my 'neighbor'?"

Jesus, ignoring this question, instead answered another which he considered much more important, "How can I be a good neighbor?" He did so subtly, with a parable, so subtly that he even got the scribe to cooperate.

"A traveler going from Jerusalem to Jericho was beaten and robbed by bandits who left him lying by the road half-dead. Soon afterward a priest came down the road and, when he saw the injured man, crossed to the other side, giving him a wide berth. Next came a Levite cleric, who did the same. Finally a Samaritan came riding by and took pity on him. After treating the man's wounds, he lifted him to his burro and took him to the nearest inn, where he continued to take care of him for the rest of the day. The next morning, before leaving to continue on his way to Jerusalem, he gave the innkeeper some money and asked him to take care of the injured man until he was well enough to leave. Further, he promised to stop at the inn on his return trip and pay the innkeeper for any additional expenses he might have incurred."

"Now which of the three men who came by on the road," Jesus asked in conclusion, "proved himself a neighbor to the injured man?"

"Why, the one who took pity on him," the scribe responded.

"Very well, then," Jesus countered, "simply behave as he did."

The Divine Shepherd

As they passed through Bethany about this time, a friend of Jesus named Martha invited them to stop at her home for dinner, and Jesus accepted her invitation. As she bustled anxiously about, trying to prepare a praiseworthy meal, her sister Mary sat quietly listening to Jesus, who evidently was in a didactic mood. After a while Martha's resentment at her sister's comfortably passive role boiled over.

"Doesn't it bother you," she interrupted to complain to Jesus, "that Mary has left me to make dinner alone? Tell her to help me."

Jesus glanced at her petulant countenance and at the elaborate meal she was preparing. If she had simply asked Mary for help, he doubtless would have kept his opinion to himself, but he was not about to act as agent for officiousness. "Martha, Martha," he answered in a tone of gentle reproach, "you worry and fret about a great many things but not about the one important thing. Mary has chosen a better course to follow, and that choice shouldn't be denied her." Martha's reaction is not recorded.

Since Bethany is very near Jerusalem, Jesus decided to pay the city a visit. On their way in, he and his companions passed a beggar who was widely known to have been blind from birth. Some of the disciples got into a weighty theological argument over why the man had been born blind; could he have committed a sin in the womb, or was he blind because of some sin of his parents? Much troubled, they asked Jesus for his opinion.

"Neither," Jesus replied. "He is blind in order to demonstrate the power of God. We must do God's work while the day lasts, before the dark of night, when his power can't be shown." Looking at the beggar compassionately, he added, "While I remain in this world, I am the light of the world." Placing a bit of clay made with spittle on the beggar's eyes, he told him to wash it off in the nearby pool of Siloam.

The beggar did so and, to his delight, found that he could see. As he walked about the pool staring eagerly about him, some people recognized him. "Isn't this the fellow who used to sit over there and beg?" After hearing the controversy, the beggar identified himself.

"How is it that you're no longer blind?" he was asked.

"The man called Jesus put some clay on my eyes," he replied, "and then told me to wash it off in the pool. I did, and now I can see."

"Where is this fellow?"

The beggar shrugged. "I don't know."

Since there were religious implications of sorts in his story, he was taken to the authorities who, of course, were shocked that anyone should make clay and restore sight on the Sabbath. Some of them, however, were troubled: "How could a sinner perform such feats?" And the beggar, when asked for an explanation, answered simply, "The man's a prophet."

The skeptics insisted on investigating further. Summoning the beggar's parents for questioning, they asked them to account for their son's recently acquired vision. But his parents, having heard of an agreement among the authorities that anyone testifying for Jesus should be excommunicated, gave wary testimony: "We know that he's our son who was born blind, but we don't know how his sight was restored or who did it. Ask him; he's of age and can speak for himself."

After dismissing them, the frustrated authorities called the beggar back and suggested to him out of their infinite wisdom that Jesus was a Sabbath-breaking sinner and thus could not have healed him.

"Whether he's a sinner I don't know," the beggar responded. "What I do know is that I was blind before and now I can see."

"Well, how did he do it?" asked his interrogators.

"I've already told you," he replied testily, "and you didn't listen to me. Do you want to hear it all over again? Why, are you thinking of becoming his disciples?"

Stung by his last question, they began verbally abusing him, accusing him of being a disciple of "that man," whereas *they* were disciples of Moses. "We know that God has spoken through Moses, but we know nothing of this fellow's origins."

"Well, that's a wonder," retorted the beggar, now thoroughly aroused. "You may know nothing of his origins, but he gave me my sight. We're told that God responds not to sinners but to those who worship and obey him. In all the world's history no one has given sight to anyone born blind. If this man weren't sent here by God, he could do nothing!"

"You were born totally in sin," came the angry reply, "and you presume to lecture us?!" And they had him thrown out of the hearing room.

When Jesus heard about this, he found the beggar and asked him, in the presence of some Pharisees, whether he believed "in the Son of God."

"Who might that be?" asked the beggar innocently. "Tell me, so that I can believe in him."

"You're looking at him," replied Jesus, "and listening to him."

"Then, Lord, I believe," the beggar responded, sinking to his knees.

"I've come into the world for this reason," Jesus continued, staring at the Pharisees, "that those without sight may see, and those who can see may go blind."

"Are we blind, then?" asked one of the Pharisees.

"If you were blind," Jesus answered wearily, "you wouldn't be guilty. But since you say you see so well, your guilt persists." In his confrontations with the authorities, he showed no eager preference for soft answers designed to turn away wrath.

"I assure you," Jesus continued, launching into one of the extended mystical metaphors that he used so often with hostile audiences, "that only thieves enter a sheepfold over the fence rather than through the gate. A keeper will open the gate for a shepherd, whose sheep will recognize his voice and follow him out to pasture, although they won't follow anyone whose voice they don't recognize."

He paused. His listeners stared at him vacantly but expectantly. And so he went on to explain, though still in metaphor.

"I am the gate. Thieves have preceded me, but the sheep have not responded to their calls. I am the gate, and whoever uses me as such can enter the sheepfold for protection and leave it for pasture. Thieves come only to steal and destroy, but I have come to keep the sheep alive and healthy.

"Or think of me as the faithful shepherd who will risk his life for his sheep. A mere hireling, to whom the sheep don't belong, will run away when a wolf appears, leaving them unprotected. But I am the good shepherd: I known mine as mine know me, even as the Father knows me and I know the Father; and I will give up my life to save the sheep.

"There are other sheep, mine also, but not in this sheepfold. They will recognize my voice, and I must bring them in to join the others in one flock, with one shepherd.

"The Father loves me because I willingly give up my life in order to receive it. I have the authority to give it up and the power to take it back again, as I have been charged by my Father."

Murmurs of dissension had been growing among his audience, which now split into two factions. One maintained that he was a madman, thoroughly possessed, who should be ignored. The others demurred, arguing that madmen didn't speak as subtly as he, nor did they restore sight to the blind. Jesus left them to settle the argument, if possible, among themselves.

I and the Father

Some time thereafter, on a winter day in Jerusalem, as Jesus was walking through the enclosed Porch of Solomon at the temple, he was surrounded by some authorities voicing impatience with his reluctance to declare flatly whether he was "the" Messiah. "How long do you intend to keep us in suspense?" he was asked. "If you're the Christ, tell us so plainly."

"I've already answered you," countered Jesus, "but you refuse to believe in me, despite the testimony of the things that I do in my Father's name. You don't believe me because you're not in my flock. My flock recognize me, as I recognize them, and they follow me. I bring them eternal life, and no one will wrest them from my grasp. My Father, who put them in my charge, possesses supreme power; no one can wrest them from his grasp. And I and the Father are one."

This last statement so infuriated some of the authorities that they began gathering stones with which to settle the argument. Jesus, unperturbed, took to tickling them with some feathers from their own duster.

"I've done many good deeds with the power from my Father; for which of these do you intend to stone me?" he asked innocently.

"These stones are not for any good deeds," came the answer, "but for blasphemy—because you, a mere man, make yourself out to be God."

"Isn't there a psalm in your Scriptures," replied Jesus, "in which men are called gods? If it called some judges gods—no, no, you can't deny your Scriptures—how can you charge blasphemy against the Father's sacred emissary for saying, 'I am the Son of God'?

"If I fail to do deeds that bear the mark of my Father, then don't believe in me. But if I do such deeds, then even if you don't believe in me, believe in them. Through them you may come to understand that the Father is in me and I am in the Father."

The little crowd pressed closer, and, in their renewed fury, some of the authorities tried to grab Jesus to prepare him for their final argument. But his time had not yet come, and once again he proved elusive.

He escaped to the place across the Jordan where John had earlier done his baptizing and stayed there awhile. Many people of the area came out to meet him. John, they conceded, had performed no wonders, but what he had said about this man had proved true. And not a few of them confessed their belief in Jesus on the spot.

The Menacing Fox

On his return from across the Jordan, Jesus was brought some news. Pontius Pilate, the Roman governor of Judea, had surprised some Galileans, whom he suspected of being rebels, while they were offering some animal sacrifices. After ordering his troops to kill them all, he then further ordered that their blood be mixed with that of the slaughtered animals, doubtless for some murkily superstitious purpose.

Jesus may have suspected that his informants were politically motivated in bringing him this news. Some may have hoped that his reaction would be seditious enough to report it to the authorities; others may have hoped that the news would incite him to lead them in a gloriously triumphant rebellion against the overwhelming power of Rome. And so Jesus avoided politics altogether, using the incident to deny the widespread belief that misfortune was necessarily the result of sinning against God.

"Do you really think," he asked, "because those Galileans suffered that fate, that they were worse sinners than others? Not so, I tell you. Indeed, without repentance, you people of Israel will suffer a like fate. And had those eighteen people who were killed when the tower at the Pool of Siloam fell on them offended God more than everyone else in Jerusalem? Not so, I tell you; without repentance, you will suffer a like fate."

"A fig tree stood in a garden," he continued, turning to a parable to stress his mission to encourage their repentance, "and the owner of the garden was disappointed to find no figs on it. He complained to his gardener that the tree had been barren for three years and ordered him to remove it to preserve the soil. But the gardener asked him to give it another year. Cultivated and properly fertilized, it might then bear fruit; but if it didn't, then it would have to be cut down." Likewise, he seemed to be saying, the people of Israel were being given another, final chance.

But this would have meant changing their ways, and their

authorities preferred the status quo. On a Sabbath day not long thereafter, while Jesus was teaching in a synagogue, a woman appeared who had been grievously ill for the past eighteen years. Unable to straighten her body, she had to walk about, as best she could, permanently bent over. As she came up to Jesus in this pitiful condition, he saw her, gently rested his hands on her shoulders for a moment, and informed her that she was now free of her infirmity. She immediately straightened up and breathed a joyous prayer of thanks to God.

The synagogue authorities' conditioned reflex was predictable, of course. Their righteously empurpled spokesman, instead of dressing Jesus down directly, harangued the congregation. "There are six days on which labor is allowed," he sternly admonished them. "Come here then if you wish to be cured, but not on the Sabbath!"

Not many things could readily anger Jesus, but pious arrogance could do it every time. "You hypocrites!" he exclaimed. "Don't you untie your ox or burro on the Sabbath and lead it to water? Then why shouldn't this woman, a daughter of Abraham, have been freed on a Sabbath day from the illness to which Satan had bound her for these past eighteen years?"

After a moment's silence, the congregation began nodding and murmuring their approval. Jesus turned and left the synagogue amid their growing acclaim and to the authorities' intense chagrin.

Yet for all his distressing impertinence, some of the authorities, if not quite his ardent friends, at least did not wish to see him murdered. Some time later a few of these came to warn him that, since Herod had murder in mind, he would do well to get out of Galilee. Jesus, though appreciating their concern for their severest critic, responded with a touch of sarcasm and more than a touch of the fatalism that seemed to be growing stronger in him with each passing day.

"You can tell that contemptible fox," he replied, with a touch of the mystical as well, "that I'll continue to exorcise and heal today and tomorrow, and on the third day my mission will be fulfilled. I must continue to my destination today and tomorrow and the next day, for surely it would be unbecoming for a prophet to perish outside the city of Jerusalem!"

To the Lions' Den

6

Jesus apparently was trying to time his final trip to Jerusalem for the feast of the Passover. That feast commemorated—with a sacrificial lamb, among other things—the passage of a people from bondage into freedom.

In any case, he continued to follow his leisurely, erratic route, now mostly in Judea, and to heal the sick and preach his subversive message. He also found time for other things, such as occasionally dining at the houses of prominent Pharisees, who seemed irrepressibly fascinated by him.

On one of these occasions he was amused by the way in which arriving guests hurried to occupy banquet places closest to the host, doubtless at the risk of some indecorous jostling. It would be better, he remarked to some of his companions (who themselves had squabbled over places in the kingdom of God), simply to go directly to the place of least honor, farthest from the host. Then, instead of perhaps being asked to give up a prized place to another and to move farther away, a guest would have no place to go but up. Thus it was, he explained (twinkling, no doubt), in the kingdom, where those who make themselves first will wind up last, and those who make themselves last will wind up first.

During dinner he was heard recommending to the host that he might sometime try giving a dinner less immersed in social custom. Instead of inviting friends and relatives and affluent neighbors, all of whom could be expected to return the favor, he might invite poor and handicapped people clearly unable to return the favor—and wait for the favor to be returned on the day of final judgment.

A guest who had overheard this, perhaps to heckle Jesus, exclaimed, "What a happy event, a banquet in the kingdom of God!"

That remark, responded Jesus, reminded him of a story. "A wealthy man once planned an elaborate banquet and sent out a great many invitations by one of his servants. But all those invited declined to come, for various reasons. One explained that he had just bought a farm and had to inspect it before closing the deal. Another had just bought five teams of oxen and was busy testing them out. Still another had just gotten married, and so on. When the servant returned without a single acceptance, his master angrily instructed him to go out in the streets and invite whatever poor and handicapped people he could find. When this failed to provide enough guests, he sent the servant out of town to scour the highways and hedges and *insist* that people come to his supper. 'My banquet will be fully attended,' he said, 'but none of those first invited will be allowed so much as a taste of it.'"

The Prodigal Son

Actually the authorities were less disturbed by his polemic table manners than by his continuing and more frequent association with tax collectors and other "sinners," and his enjoying meals with them. On one occasion, when an indignant pooh-bah criticized this disreputable habit, Jesus took the opportunity for another discourse on the value of repentant sinners.

"Suppose a woman has ten coins of great value," he suggested, "and loses one of them. Surely she'll take a lamp and search the house thoroughly until she finds it. And when she does find it, she'll probably let her neighbors know, so that they can share her relief and joy. Well, such is the joy in heaven over a sinner who has repented."

"There's a story," he continued, "of a younger son who one day asked his father to give him his share of the family inheritance. The father agreed and divided his property between his two sons. Shortly thereafter the younger son took his share and went off to a distant land, where he quickly spent it all in wild living. At that time the land was in the grip of a famine, so that he soon was not only destitute but also starving. He did find a job as a swineherd but was given very little to eat and wasn't even allowed to supplement his meager diet with so much as a mouthful of pig fodder, though he'd have gladly gulped it down.

"His predicament gave rise to fond thoughts of his former life, stirring up visions of the mouth-watering meals that his father's hired hands must even then be enjoying, while he was here envying the pigs. So he decided to return home and confess his sin against both heaven and his father, and ask for a job as a hired hand, since he had proved himself so unworthy as a son.

"When he was still some distance from the family farm, his father recognized him despite the distance and his bedraggled appearance and, moved with pity, ran and embraced him and gave him a loving kiss of welcome.

"'Father,' said the son, 'I have sinned against heaven and against you, and I'm no longer worthy to be called your son.'

"But his father, refusing to hear any more of such talk, told his servants to dress his son in the best finery and to prepare a fine meal, complete with fatted calf, in celebration. 'My son was dead,' he cried, 'but is alive again. He was lost but has been found.' And soon the house was ringing with a joyous party.

"Meanwhile the older son was returning from the fields after a hard day's work. As he approached the house, he could hear music and the sounds of dancing. Passing by a servant, he asked what was going on, and the servant replied that his father had ordered a celebration of his younger son's safe and sound return. This news so angered the older son that he stayed sullenly outside the house until finally his father emerged and entreated him to join the party.

"'Not I,' retorted the son. 'I have served you faithfully and obediently all these many years; yet you've never thrown such a party for me and my friends. But now that your younger son has returned from wasting his life on harlots, look what you've done for him!'

"'Son,' the father replied gently, 'you're always close to my heart, and all that I have is yours. But it's only right to be happy over your brother's return. He was dead, but now he's alive again. He was lost, but he's been found.'"

The Perils of Wealth

During his visit in the Pharisee's house, Jesus may have been concerned that his disciples might draw a false inference from his association with (among others) people of conspicuous wealth and consumption. A widely held notion existed then, as it does today, that wealth meant personal superiority, including spiritual superiority—a notion prevalent among poor and rich alike. He could hardly let his disciples think that he agreed with it. Their expectations were suspect enough as it was. And so, chiefly addressing his disciples, he slipped a couple of parables into the conversation.

"The manager of a wealthy man's estate was accused of

extravagance. The owner, after inspecting his ledgers, gave him notice of dismissal. The manager, recognizing that he had grown too soft to dig ditches and was too proud to beg, devised a plan to ingratiate himself with some prospective employers. Conferring with each of the owner's debtors with whom he had regularly done business, he reduced the amount owed on each contract. One debtor, for instance, reported a debt of a thousand gallons of oil; the manager changed it to five hundred. Another reported a debt of a thousand bushels of wheat; the manager dropped it to eight hundred. And so on. When the owner got wind of these arrangements, he was so taken with the manager's ingenious foresight that he congratulated him.

"The worldly-wise are indeed more cunning than you who incline to the spiritual. You would do well to use money, however worthless in itself, to be generous and thus make friends for eternity.

"A person who behaves with integrity in minor matters will normally do so in important matters, and a person who has no scruples in minor matters will normally have none in important matters. So if you fail to handle so worthless a thing as money conscientiously, who can be expected to trust you with something of real value? And if you prove untrustworthy in handling something on loan from another, who can be expected to give you something of value for your own?"

The authorities, who respected wealth and what they considered it signified, snorted and ridiculed him for such idealistic talk. Their reaction, of course, didn't faze him in the least. "You're the kind who exalt themselves before others," he retorted, "but God can read your hearts. Much that people hold dear in this world is of no value in his eyes. The old Law and the words of the Prophets held sway until the coming of John the Baptist, but now the Good News of the kingdom of God is being announced, and everyone must turn sharply to enter that kingdom."

"Let me tell you another story," he continued. "This one is about a rich man who spent an easy life dressed in purple splendor and fine linen and sated with sumptuous food and drink at every meal. All this was in contrast with the life of a disease-ridden beggar named Lazarus, who waited each day at the gate of the rich man's estate, vainly hoping for scraps from the groaning table and fending off dogs attracted by his festering sores. After both men had died, the rich man looked up from Hades and saw Lazarus in heaven.

"'Father Abraham,' he cried, 'have mercy on me. Send Lazarus to me, so that he can place a drop of cooling water on my tongue, for this fire is agony.'

"'My son,' replied Abraham, 'remember what blessings and comforts you received in your lifetime, while Lazarus was in misery. Now your roles are reversed, and you are separated by a great divide that none can cross.'

"'Then I beg you,' implored the rich man, 'to send him to my father's house to warn my five brothers, lest they wind up here also.'

"'No,' answered Abraham, 'let them listen to the warnings of Moses and the other prophets.'

"'But Father Abraham,' the rich man argued, 'if someone brings them a message from the grave, they'll repent of their sins!'

"Abraham, however, remained unmoved. 'If they won't heed the warnings of Moses and the others,' he replied, 'neither will they be persuaded by someone risen from the dead.'"

Resurrection and Alarm

Among Jesus' dearest personal friends were Martha and Mary of Bethany and their brother Lazarus. One day, Jesus, who had again left Judea to avoid the long and unfriendly arm of authority, received word from the sisters that Lazarus had fallen seriously ill. His reaction was that this was not a final illness (though he evidently knew better) but was rather an occasion for promoting the glory of God and his Son. And so, quite deliberately, he stayed where he was for a couple of days before suggesting to his disciples that they return to Judea for a visit to Bethany.

The disciples responded to the suggestion with considerable alarm. The authorities in Judea, they pointed out, still had a supply of stones with his name on them. Did he really mean to go back there now?

Yes, he did, Jesus replied, because he must continue with his mission right up to his hour of darkness. Until then he would be safe: "A man walking in the daylight will not stumble; but in the dark of night, he will."

"Anyway," he added, "our friend Lazarus is ill and has fallen asleep, and I must go and wake him up."

The disciples seized the opportunity to reassure Jesus that a visit to Judea, therefore, was really unnecessary. "If he's fallen asleep," one of them replied, either witlessly or wittily, "the sleep will do him good, and he'll recover."

"Lazarus is dead," retorted Jesus, abandoning metaphor. "And I'm happy for your sake that I wasn't there when he died, so that now your faith can be strengthened. Now, let's be on our way."

The disciples still hesitated, uneasily discussing the hazards of the visit, until finally Thomas—the apostle whose other doubts, on a later occasion, were to bring him lasting fame—shrugged his shoulders. "Well, then, let's go," he urged the others, "and die along with him."

It was not until four days after the funeral that they arrived on the outskirts of Bethany, where Martha had come out to meet them. Her house was full of funeral guests from nearby Jerusalem, she explained, and she had wanted to greet Jesus at first by herself. Mary was waiting for them back at the house.

"If you had been here," Martha gently reproached him, "he wouldn't have died." After a pause, as though harboring a hope that she dared not express, she added, "Yet I know that even now God will grant whatever you ask."

"But he will rise and live again," Jesus reassured her.

"Yes, I know," she replied, sadly taking his remark as merely a conventional reassurance. "He will rise and live again in the final resurrection."

"But I am that resurrection and that life," said Jesus. "Whoever has faith in me will live, despite death, forever. Do you believe that?"

"Yes, I do, Lord," replied Martha fervently. "I have long believed you to be the Christ, the Son of God, sent by him into the world."

Perhaps sensing that Jesus had not come to enjoy a social gathering at her house, she went back for Mary. When she returned, it was not only with Mary but also with a large contingent of guests who apparently thought that the two sisters had left the house to visit their brother's tomb.

Mary, unable to control her grief, fell at Jesus' feet and repeated Martha's reproach, "If only you had been here, he wouldn't have died."

She burst into tears, as did Martha and many of the guests. Jesus, deeply moved, asked where Lazarus was buried. As they led him to the tomb, there were tears in his eyes, too. Some of the guests, noticing this, remarked on how much he had loved his friend. Others, however, recalling Mary's greeting, commented that surely someone who had given sight to the blind could have saved his dear friend from death.

When they arrived at the tomb, which consisted of a burial cave closed with a slab of stone, Jesus, his voice unsteady with emotion, asked that the stone be removed.

"But by now," protested the ever-practical Martha, "the stench would be overpowering. He's been dead for four days!"

"Haven't I told you," answered Jesus, "that if you have faith, you'll see the glory of God?"

After the stone had been moved away, he lifted his eyes and prayed, "Father, I thank you for hearing me. I know that you always do hear me, but now I pray for this aloud so that the people here may believe that I'm your messenger." Then, in a strong voice, he called, "Lazarus, come out!"

The hush that settled over the crowd ended in gasps of surprise as Lazarus appeared, his body swathed in burial wrappings, his face covered with a scarf.

"Take off the wrappings," Jesus ordered matter-of-factly, "and let him go free."

Though all shared in the general astonishment, the crowd reacted with mixed emotions. Many declared their belief in Jesus on the spot, while others hurried back to Jerusalem to report the incident to the authorities.

The authorities, deeply disturbed by the report, immediately called a council to discuss strategy. Jesus' wonder working was impressive enough to attract the unwelcome attention of the Romans, who took a dim view of anything resembling civil unrest or disorder. They might deprive the council members of their treasured authority, and might even divest Judea of what little sovereignty it had.

It was a brief speech by Caiaphas, the high priest, that decided Jesus' fate. "Can't you see what's involved?" he asked his colleagues impatiently. "It's to your advantage that one man die for the people to prevent the ruin of the whole community." From that point on, the council discussed strategy solely in terms of how best to put Jesus to death.

When Jesus got wind of this, he left the vicinity of Jerusalem and retired for a while to a remote village called Ephraim at the edge of the wilderness, but only for a while.

The Second Coming

From Ephraim, Jesus and company wandered northward, coming one day to a village from which a group of ten lepers came out to meet them. Standing at some distance to one side of the road, they called to him, begging him to have pity on them. Jesus, in his characteristically unsentimental way, simply told them to go to the local priests for the physical examination that the law required before they could be declared "clean."

They did so, and were so declared. Now they could be received back into the community. In their great delight they rushed off to their various homes to join their loved ones again. But one, a Samaritan whose home may have been some distance away, returned to Jesus, fell at his feet and thanked him, with heartfelt praise for the power of God.

Glancing at the nearest of his disciples, Jesus asked wryly, "Weren't there ten who were healed? Where could the other nine be? Is this foreigner the only one to return and praise God?" Then, turning to the Samaritan and lifting him to his feet, he said, "Please get up and go on your way. Your faith has made you whole again."

This incident and its attendant publicity seems to have flushed up a covey of Pharisees, who came to him requesting a specific date for the coming of the kingdom of God. They may have hoped that he would commit himself to an early date, which they might then report to the Roman authorities, together with an alarming political interpretation.

Once again Jesus showed his inability to take such devious boobies seriously. "The kingdom of God," he replied sardonically, "won't come simply from looking for it. There won't be people calling out, 'Oops, here it is!' or 'Hey, look, it's over there!' The kingdom of God is within."

After the frustrated Pharisees had left, he continued the discussion with his disciples but in another vein. The subject now was his own mysterious, mystical "Second Coming," which he may have hoped would occur soon after his death, but which he could never predict with any assurance.

"There'll come a time," he told them, "when you'll want to see just one day of the Son of man, but you won't see it. And people will indeed say things like 'Here, we see it,' or 'Look, over there!' But pay them no mind: as lightning flashing from one direction lights up the whole sky, so will it be with the Son of man when his day comes. But first he must undergo much suffering and be rejected by this generation.

"As it was in Noah's time, so will it be in the Son of man's time. The people of that time kept on eating and drinking and getting married until the day that Noah entered the ark, and the flood caught them unawares. So it was, too, in the land of Sodom: they ate and drank, they bought and sold, they planted and built until the day that Lot fled the city, and the fire and brimstone caught and destroyed them. That's the unexpected way it will be when the Son of man is finally revealed.

"On that day, whoever is on the roof need not go back down into the house to rescue any belongings, and whoever is out in the fields may as well stay there. Remember Lot's wife! Indeed, whoever then bends all his or her effort to saving the life he or she knows will lose it, but whoever willingly gives it up will have life forever. Friendship will count as nothing: of two men together in a field, one will be taken and the other left behind, and of two women grinding grain together, one will be taken and the other left behind."

Understandably confused, the disciples could think of nothing better to ask than where all this would happen, despite what he had already said about its not being "here" or "there." In his enigmatic reply, Jesus seemed to be saying that the answer would be clear enough when the day finally arrived: "Wherever the carcass is, there will the vultures be gathered."

Thus they would have to be patient and not lose heart. Reassuring them, he changed the subject to the power of perseverance in prayer, offering them a little entertainment in the form of a parable.

"There was a judge in a certain city," he told them, "who neither feared God nor had any regard for other people. A widow in the same city who was undergoing some legal harassment kept pestering him to obtain some relief for her, but he kept putting her off. She persisted, however, until finally he said to himself, 'I neither fear God nor concern myself with other people, but this woman is giving me so much trouble that I'll have to give her a satisfactory judgment before she completely wears me out.'

"Consider his reaction, and then tell me, if you can, that God, who has been so patient with his chosen people, won't answer those who pester him day and night with prayer. I assure you, he will respond, and soon. But, when the Son of man returns, will he find on earth the faith needed for such perseverance?"

On Pride in Hearts and Husbands

On another occasion Jesus offered a parable for those with a high opinion of themselves, bolstered by a self-righteous contempt for others. "Two men," he said, "went into the temple to pray. One was a Pharisee, the other a tax collector. The Pharisee, standing meticulously apart from the common folk, prayed privately with these words: 'God, I thank you that I'm not like others, people guilty of extortion, injustices, adultery, and even tax collecting. I fast twice a week, more often than required, and I give tithes of all my income, not just some of it.'

"In contrast, the tax collector, standing diffidently in the background, kept his eyes cast downward and struck his breast in self-accusation. 'O God,' he prayed, 'be merciful to me, a sinner.' Let me tell you, it was he, and not the other, who went home absolved in the sight of God."

Not long thereafter, some Pharisees of theologically sportive bent approached him for another sparring match. These particular authorities could not very well have been among those who had already resolved to end the Jesus problem with a final solution, especially since their question had no political implications. It was related rather to a solemn rabbinical controversy raging at the time over whether a wife could lawfully be put aside, or divorced, only for adultery or for a less serious reason like burning the toast (literally).

"Is it lawful," the Pharisees' spokesman therefore asked, "for a man to put aside his wife for any trivial reason?"

As Jesus demonstrated throughout his public life, a question solemnly asked need not be solemnly answered. Again he referred his questioners to the Scriptures on which they were such experts. "Haven't you ever read that God created human beings as male and female and declared that a man leaves his parents in marrying his wife and that the couple then become as one body? The two of them are one, and what God has thus joined together no one should force apart."

"But then," one heckler retorted, "why did Moses allow bills of divorce, permitting a husband to put his wife aside?"

The question was put rather triumphantly, but Jesus was never fazed by slavish appeals to authority. "He did so," he answered evenly, "to accommodate the hard attitudes of those harsh times, but that wasn't the original arrangement.

"I tell you again, a man who puts a faithful wife aside, and who marries another woman, is committing adultery. And a man who marries a wife so put aside also is committing adultery, as is the woman."

This apparently left the Pharisees out of their depth, but some of the disciples found Jesus' remarks quite alarming. "If a man has this kind of responsibility toward his wife," one of them exclaimed, "then surely it's smarter not to get married at all!"

"Now *that* advice," smiled Jesus, "is not for everyone, but only for those who can take it. There are those who are born impotent and others who are made impotent. Still others in effect make themselves impotent to devote themselves wholly to establishing the kingdom of God. Whoever finds such advice to be practicable may follow it."

These remarks on marriage are immediately followed in the

record, perhaps significantly, by the report of an incident in which some small children were brought to Jesus with a request that he bestow on them a protective touch and prayer. Some of the disciples resisted this with some choice epithets, presumably on the grounds that Jesus was too busy. Jesus, however, indignantly demanded that they let the children be brought to him. "It is the likes of them that make up the kingdom of God," he exclaimed. "Whoever fails to accept the kingdom with the heart of a child will also fail to enter it." Then he embraced and blessed them and, with his disciples, continued on his way.

The Rewards of Detachment

In the next town they passed through, a wealthy young aristocrat came to Jesus and asked him, with perhaps too elaborate a show of respect, "Good rabbi, what should I do to inherit eternal life?"

"Why do you call me good," Jesus asked, not irrelevantly, "when only God is good? You know his commandments: you must not kill nor commit adultery, steal nor bear false witness; you must honor your father and mother, and so on."

"But I have observed these commandments all my life," the young man responded, clearly disappointed in such unimaginative counsel. "Isn't there anything more?"

"Since you ask," replied Jesus sharply but affectionately, "there is a little something more if you're looking for perfection: sell all that you own, give the proceeds to the poor—this will earn you wealth in heaven—and follow me."

Shocked and saddened, the young aspirant turned away. He couldn't bring himself to accept the advice he had asked for, since he was a very rich young man, indeed.

Jesus, too, was saddened as he watched him depart. "I must say," he commented dryly to his disciples, "it's hard for the rich to enter the kingdom of God, harder than for a camel to squeeze itself through the eye of a needle."

The disciples were stunned by such heretical talk. In their culture it was almost a truism, assiduously nurtured by many authorities, that wealth and status in this life were a sign of similar felicities in the next. "Then who," one of them stammered, "can possibly be saved?"

"No human power alone can bring salvation," Jesus smiled, "but God can do anything."

"How about us?" asked Peter in anxious self-reference. "We have given up everything to follow you."

"Anyone who has left country, home, or family for me and my

message," Jesus reassured him, "will be rewarded many times over in eternal life."

He did not, however, intend to encourage any competitive anxiety over proportionate rewards, and so he offered his disciples a cautionary tale. "The kingdom of heaven," he told them, "reminds me of the owner of a vineyard who went out at dawn one morning to hire some workers. In the nearby village he found some men who agreed to work that day in his vineyard for the customary daily wage. After getting them started, he went out again about nine o'clock and hired some more, and then did the same at noon and at about three o'clock. Late in the afternoon, still needing more workers, he returned to the village about five o'clock and, finding some men standing about idly in the marketplace, asked them why they weren't working. When they replied that it was because no one had hired them, he took them back to work in the vineyard, even though it was only an hour before quitting time.

"Well, when the working day was over, he instructed his manager to pay each of the workers a day's wages. Thus those who'd been hired at five o'clock received as much pay as those who'd been hired at dawn. The full-day workers, in discussing this, worked themselves up into a considerable froth over their laboring all day in the scorching sun for no more pay than the others were getting for a single comfortable hour. They appointed a spokesman, who complained about it bitterly to the vineyard owner.

"'My friend,' answered the owner, 'I did you no injustice. Didn't you agree with me on a day's work for a day's wages? So please take your rightful pay and leave. Haven't I a right to distribute what's mine as I think best? Have you any right to look on my generosity with such an envious eye?'"

A Role for Authority

As the time for Jesus' final visit to Jerusalem approached, his wandering began to take a more direct heading toward that city. The disciples, noticing this, began to grow nervous again. Although most were quite confident of his eventual triumph, they preferred to hedge their bets. Going to Jerusalem now, they felt, involved an uncomfortable degree of risk. They favored a less precarious conquest, to be undertaken after the present dust had settled.

Jesus clearly felt that he should make another attempt to disabuse them of the idea that he expected to take Jerusalem the way Joshua took Jericho. Taking the twelve apostles aside, he confirmed that they were indeed headed for Jerusalem, where "the predictions of the prophets about the Son of man will be fulfilled. He will be delivered to the authorities, both Jewish and Gentile, and will be humiliated, scourged, condemned to death and executed—and three days later will rise from the grave."

He may as well have saved his breath. So little did they get of the picture that shortly afterward the apostles James and John privately approached him with a request that they be assigned, in his kingdom, the foremost places of honor and authority, "one of us at your right hand, the other at your left."

Jesus concealed most of his anger and chagrin with a metaphor. "Will you be able," he asked them severely, "to drink from the cup that I'm about to drink from?"

They eagerly, if ignorantly, assured him that they would.

"You will do so, indeed," he promised them with sardonic sorrow. "But as for the places at my right and my left, they are already reserved."

When the other apostles caught the scent of their colleagues' sneaky political maneuvering, they expressed their resentful choler in choice and specific terms. Jesus, painfully disturbed by their ludicrous jostling, tried once again to infuse in his apostles, his select Twelve, some understanding of what he meant by honor and authority.

"You know how it is among the Gentiles," he said, "how their authorities lord it over the people. That's not the way it should be among you. Whoever wants to be outstanding among you must serve all the others. The Son of man himself has come into this world not to be served but to serve and to offer his life as a ransom for others."

A Stopover in Jericho

Only two towns, Jericho and Bethany, now remained between Jesus and Jerusalem. As he and his followers came to the outskirts of Jericho, the noise of their talking and shuffling along the road attracted the attention of a blind roadside beggar named Timaeus. When he asked someone what was going on, he was told that the prophet Jesus, of Nazareth, was passing by.

"Jesus, Son of David," he cried out, "have pity on me!" Several bystanders, in whose superior sight his lack of dignity may have been offensive, tried to shush him, but he persisted with the same cry (including the artful honorific) until finally Jesus stopped and asked what he wanted.

"O Lord," he shouted back excitedly, "that I may *see!*" Flinging off the burden of his cloak, he groped his way to Jesus, who gazed on him sympathetically and said, "Your faith has healed you."

Suddenly he could see. And Jesus had another disciple.

As they were passing through the streets of Jericho, a man named Zacchaeus, an important and quite wealthy tax collector, walked some distance from his house to catch a glimpse of the celebrated healer. He was a very short man, however, and found that all he could see was the closely packed crowd at about waist level. But he also found out that Jesus and company would soon be passing by his house, near which stood a convenient sycamore tree. Reaching his property and hoisting himself into the tree, he waited. Jesus appeared and, to Zacchaeus's surprise, called him by name.

"Come down, Zacchaeus," Jesus called, grinning amiably, "and be quick about it. I'm going to be visiting you for a little while." Highly flattered, Zacchaeus clambered down from his perch and welcomed his unexpected guest enthusiastically while pious lip pursers in the crowd clucked their disapproval at Jesus' accepting the hospitality of such a sinner.

Zacchaeus, embarrassed by the clucking and impressed by Jesus' affability, assured him that he would turn over new leaves in great quantity. "I promise you, Rabbi," he exclaimed, "I'll distribute half my wealth to the poor, and if I've wrongfully taken anything from anyone, I'll make a fourfold restoration."

Now it was Jesus' turn to be impressed. "Salvation has come to this house today," he told his disciples, "since this man will now behave as a son of Abraham should. Remember that the Son of man has come to find the lost and to save them."

During his stay in Jericho, Jesus may have been mulling over the apostles' jealous concern over rank in the kingdom of God and over their evident assumption that the kingdom was awaiting them just around the next corner. Indeed, they even seemed to feel that the imminent visit to Jerusalem might inaugurate it. Although by his own admission he didn't know when the kingdom (including his own "Second Coming") would arrive, he apparently felt that he should warn his followers—and, through them, *their* followers to come— that they all might be in for a long wait. And that in the meantime they would be responsible for conducting themselves by the rules he had given them—for returning their gifts from God, as it were, with interest.

This, at any rate, may explain why he chose this time to tell his disciples a parable which is reminiscent of a historical incident of some years earlier. After the death of Herod the Great, his son Archelaus traveled to Rome to ask Augustus Caesar to appoint him king. A deputation of some fifty Jews was sent from Palestine to oppose his petition, and, as a result, Augustus made him governor of only half of Herod's kingdom. It is surprising that Jesus would have told a story with such political overtones. And yet—

"A certain nobleman," he told his disciples, "made plans to visit a distant country, to receive (he hoped) a kingdom from his overlord, and then to return. Before leaving, in a meeting with his servants, he gave three of them equal sums of money, instructing them to multiply their trusts as best they could in commercial transactions during his absence. Soon after he left, some citizens sent a deputation to the overlord to protest his appointment, though to no avail.

"On his return, in another meeting, after announcing the success of his trip, he called the three servants to account. The first eagerly turned over to him the original sum plus ten times as much; the newly appointed king congratulated him and gave him charge of ten cities in his new realm. The second reported similar success, though only to the extent of adding five times as much, and he was given charge of five cities.

"The third servant, however, returned only the original sum, carefully wrapped in a napkin. 'I kept it safe like this,' he tried to explain, 'because I was afraid of your reputation for severe dealing, for taking what you haven't earned, and for reaping what you haven't sown.'

"'You incompetent dolt!' cried the master. 'Your own report condemns you! If you knew my reputation so well, why didn't you at least put the money securely in a bank, so that you could return it to me with interest?' And he ordered that the man's money be taken from him and given to the first servant.

"Then, as if to confirm his reputation further, he ordered the rebellious local leaders, who had protested his appointment, to be brought before him and executed on the spot."

A Farewell Party

In Bethany, at the house of a cured leper named Simon, a supper party was given in Jesus' honor. It seems to have been a rather elaborate affair. Some of his disciples and other friends were there, including Lazarus and his sisters Martha and Mary—with Martha, not surprisingly, officiating as hostess and volunteer factotum. Apparently, some of the irrepressibly optimistic disciples had bruited it about that Jesus was going to Jerusalem to inaugurate his kingdom, and the party thus was given partly to honor a soon-to-be king.

This became fairly clear when Mary approached Jesus after

supper with an alabaster jar containing an expensive perfumed ointment. Soon the air was filled with the scent of perfume as she went about anointing him in a fashion reminiscent of Old Testament coronations, leaving Jesus with a choice between angry protest and good-natured tolerance. He chose the latter.

The brief ceremony was barely completed when Judas Iscariot, the company treasurer and a man suspected of having sticky fingers, complained to Mary, "Why wasn't this ointment sold? It would have brought a sizable sum which could have been given to the poor."

Although Jesus may have been in general agreement with the principle behind this ungracious comment, he rose to Mary's defense. "Why badger her?" he asked Judas reproachfully. "The poor will be with you always, but I am soon to leave you. Indeed," he continued with a wry smile, "she has anointed me for death. Let her keep the rest of the ointment for my burial. Wherever my message is preached, she'll be remembered for this."

Meanwhile crowds had been gathering around the house to see not only Jesus but also Lazarus, whose return from the grave had been widely reported. In fact, his very existence had become such a cause for popular belief in Jesus that the authorities had decided on *his* elimination as well.

Defeat 7

The authorities had good reason to include Lazarus in their homicidal plans. His story, still a topic of lively conversation among the people of Jerusalem, seems to have been largely responsible for the spectacular welcome given Jesus as he entered the city. Magicians of this time were credited with many wonders, but not with recalling people from the grave. Jesus had earned himself a very special reputation and a very special welcome.

As he approached the city with his disciples, he sent two of them ahead to find a burro at a certain place and bring it back to him. They would be allowed to take it, he assured them, if they simply said it was for him, and so it turned out. The prophet Zechariah, it was generally believed, had predicted that the Messiah would enter Jerusalem riding on such an animal, and Jesus doubtless had this in mind. This kind of arrival, besides its messianic intimations, should also imply that any attempt at "conquest" would be a peaceable one. A military hero would consider a burro too far beneath his dignity.

Jesus was nonetheless greeted with loud acclaim by crowds of people waving palm branches in celebration, laying their cloaks on the ground in his path as a token of respect, and shouting their welcome "to the son of David" and "to the king who comes in the name of the Lord." Some authorities in the crowd, as Jesus passed by them, urged him to reprimand his disciples for allowing the demonstration to get out of hand, but Jesus answered them with a paraphrase from Scripture. "If these people are silenced," he shot back, "the stones along the way will do the shouting."

Late that afternoon, after the people had quieted down and he and his companions had visited the temple in relative peace, they went out to the nearby Mount of Olives and looked down on the city. Tears came to Jesus' eyes as he gazed upon it, for he loved it and feared for it. "O Jerusalem," he murmured sadly, "if only you recognized, even now, what can bring you peace! The day will come when your enemies will encompass and besiege you, grind you to rubble, and destroy your people. They'll not leave one stone upon another, because you failed to see your opportunity."

The next morning, as the disciples and Jesus were returning to the city, a curious incident occurred. As they passed a fig tree standing by the road, Jesus, complaining of hunger, went up to it to pluck a few figs. Finding plenty of inedible leaves but not a single fig, he cursed it with uncharacteristic petulance: "From now on may you never bear any fruit!" And immediately the tree dried up and lost its leaves.

If he did this to demonstrate the power of faith again to his disciples, whose faith was to be sorely tested in Jerusalem, he was successful. They were properly impressed, and this gave him another opportunity to recommend the faith that can move mountains. But this time he added a caveat: "If anyone has offended you, pray in a forgiving spirit, so that your Father in heaven may forgive you for offending *him*."

Trouble in the Temple

They entered the city and went directly to the temple, where Jesus once again forcibly expelled the traders and the money changers who seemed persistently intent on transforming the temple precincts into a tumultuous bazaar. On this occasion, he and his disciples seem to have dominated temple activities; for instance, they prevented the temple area from being used as a shortcut. The temple priests were livid, of course, but the obvious and practically unanimous support that Jesus was receiving from the people gave them incentive to bide their time.

After things had quieted down and Jesus had resumed his healing and preaching, a priestly delegation came to him and, as they had before, indignantly demanded that he tell them by what authority he did such outrageous things. The question was rhetorical, since they knew in their hearts that he had no authority whatsoever, and Jesus treated it as such.

"Let me ask you a question," he slyly countered, "and if you answer it, I'll tell you by what authority I do these things: what was the authority behind John's baptisms; was it divine or merely human?"

A couple of them confidently started to answer but were restrained by some of their cannier colleagues, who quickly recognized that his question left them in an uncomfortable predicament. If they answered "divine," they muttered in a hasty conference, Jesus then could ask why they had refused to believe John, thus severely embarrassing them before the large and attentive crowd. If they answered "human," the crowd, who, they knew, accepted John as a genuine prophet, might grow violent and start throwing things. (Stones seem always to have been readily available for arguments in the temple area.) Squirming helplessly in the vise, they could think of no better answer than "We can't tell."

"Very well," Jesus replied, smiling grimly, "then neither will I tell you by what authority I do these things."

"Consider this story," he continued, drawing on an ancient Hebrew parable. "A man with two sons asked one of them to work that day in his vineyard. The son at first refused but later reconsidered and did work through the day in the vineyard. After this son refused, the man made the same request of his other son, who readily agreed but then spent the day quietly avoiding the vineyard. Which of the two sons, would you say, did as the father wanted?"

"The first one, of course," someone answered.

"Let me tell you," said Jesus, staring at the cluster of priests, "whores and tax collectors will enter the kingdom of heaven before you do. John brought you words of justice, yet it was such as they, not you, who believed him, and you haven't even now repented of your disbelief." He paused a moment while his would-be hecklers fidgeted in their uneasy but discreet silence.

"Here's another story for you," he went on mercilessly. "Another man, who also owned a vineyard, rented it out to sharecroppers and left the country. When the time came to collect his share, he sent a servant back for it, but the sharecroppers beat the servant up and sent him back empty-handed. The owner sent another servant, whom they treated likewise, and then another and another; he sent a veritable procession of servants, whom the sharecroppers mistreated, injured, and, in some cases, even killed. Finally the owner sent his son, whom he loved dearly; he never thought that they would harm his son. But in the son, when he came to them, they saw an opportunity to take over the vineyard for themselves, and so they hauled him out and killed him."

He paused again while some of the priests glared at him.

"After that, what would you expect the owner to do?" Jesus challenged them. "What else would he do but come back and eliminate the sharecroppers and turn the vineyard over to others?" Then, alluding to a biblical psalm with which he knew they'd be acquainted, he continued, "Surely you've read this in Scripture: 'The stone that the builders rejected has now become the cornerstone.'"

While murmurs of approval rose from the crowd, the priests, enraged by his innuendo, retreated with as much dignity as their frustration would allow.

In No Uncertain Terms

The authorities may have been frustrated by losing so many battles to this slippery, subversive upstart, but they were determined to win the war. During the next several days they kept after him in relays—probing, testing, needling, persistently trying to get him to say something that they could use to his terminal regret.

On one occasion, for instance, some Pharisees got together with some Herodians and devised a little scheme for trapping Jesus into a hazardous dilemma. They would ask him whether the Jews should pay Roman taxes. If he answered "yes," he would probably lose the confidence of most of his Jewish followers; if he answered "no," he could be reported, eagerly, to the Roman governor, Pontius Pilate.

To throw him off guard, their spokesman introduced their question with a flattering little preamble. "Rabbi," he fawned, "we recognize that you're a man of integrity and a teacher of truth, unawed by human authority. So give us your opinion: is it right for us to pay taxes to Caesar, or not?"

Jesus grinned at the man's elaborately earnest expression and decided on a similarly elaborate response. "Why do you pull such tricks on me, you sly rascals?" he answered, surveying the unfriendly clique. "Give me one of the coins used to pay these taxes."

After some fumbling about, an imperial silver coin was found and handed to him. Turning it about in his hand, he gazed at it curiously, as though he had never seen one before, and then asked with studied innocence, "Whose likeness is this stamped on it, and whose name?"

Some of them by now must have suspected that he was playing a game, but they could think of no better reply than the truth. "Why, Caesar's," answered their spokesman.

"Why, then," said Jesus, as solemnly as he could, "if this is Caesar's, you should give back to Caesar whatever is Caesar's, and give to God whatever is God's."

Their only response, the record tells us, was an embarrassed silence and grudging admiration.

A later deputation was made up of Sadducean priests who had another catchy puzzler for him, this one a theological poser apparently designed to test his religious rather than his political orthodoxy. One of the Sadducees' general fixations was the belief (held by the Pharisees) in the eventual physical resurrection of the dead, which they maintained could not be justified from the Scriptures. So, in their question to Jesus, they attacked this belief by reducing it to an absurdity.

"Rabbi," a spokesman put it to him, "Moses decreed that if a man died childless, his brother should inseminate his widow, to give him children. Now we give you a case of seven bachelor brothers. The first died childless, so the second married his widow. Then the second died childless and the third married her, and so on until finally the seventh died childless; after that the widow died. Now if there's a resurrection, which of the brothers would be considered her husband?" One can easily imagine the satisfied smirks accompanying this thorny, thorny conundrum.

But Jesus was not so easily led into imprisoning thickets. These people spent their lives debating such trifling questions in bottomless holes, but he had other things to do. Further, he knew the practical side of the Mosaic Law better than they did.

"Perhaps the reason you're so addicted to error," he answered flatly, "is your ignorance of both Scripture and the power of God. People marry in the world, but after the resurrection the children of God will enjoy eternal life without marriage, like the angels do.

"As for the resurrection of the dead," he continued, addressing himself to their central question, though very obliquely, "how is it that God, in the Scriptures, spoke of himself to Moses as the God of Abraham, Isaac, and Jacob? Since these patriarchs are still alive in spirit, he is the God not of the dead but of the living. You couldn't be more wrong."

The Sadducees were so taken aback by his assertiveness, it seems, that they simply nodded in weak agreement. And so they left the arena for the time being.

The next relay team consisted of some Pharisees, who brought along a legal scholar to spearhead their attack. He quickly proved to be an unusual fellow, in whom some wisdom had survived under the burden of his scholarship. Instead of badgering Jesus with some arcane trifle, he got right down to fundamentals—possibly because he thought so novel an approach would throw Jesus off balance.

"Rabbi," he asked respectfully, "which is the most important of the commandments of God?"

This, for a change, was a question that Jesus could treat seriously. "The first," he answered, "is to love the Lord your God with all your heart and soul, all your mind and strength. The second is to love your neighbor as you love yourself. There are no commandments more important than these."

"Rabbi," replied the lawyer, his respect suddenly more genuine, "I can hardly quarrel with your answer. God is indeed one God, and loving him with all our heart and mind and strength, together with loving our neighbor as ourselves, means more to him than all the smoldering sacrifices ever offered."

Jesus smiled warmly. The respect was mutual. "My friend," he said, "you're not far from the kingdom of God."

Since the Pharisees clearly had no further questions, Jesus decided to go on the offensive with a riddle of the kind they seemed to enjoy so much. "What's your opinion about the Messiah?" he asked them. "From whom is he supposed to be descended?"

"Why, from David," one of them replied. "He is called the son of David."

"Then how is it," asked Jesus, referring to a biblical psalm, "that David, inspired by the Holy Spirit, spoke of the Messiah as his Lord when he sang, 'The Lord God said to my Lord, "Sit at my right hand until I cast your enemies at your feet"'? If David thus called the Messiah his Lord, how could the Messiah be merely his son?"

The Pharisees retreated. They had neither an answer nor any further questions, and they may have wanted to find themselves another lawyer.

These few examples constitute only a small sample of the incessant heckling that Jesus must have put up with during the first part of his stay in Jerusalem. He seems to have fended off these public inquisitions with skill and good humor, but the arrogant, hypocritical approach used so often by the authorities and their agents finally emptied his enormous reservoir of tolerance. And so one day, while talking to some of his disciples amid a crowd of onlookers, he launched into a diatribe against his foes among the authorities, a tirade more virulent than any speech of his made before or afterward. It was so strong that it has become famous.

"It is true," he conceded at the outset, "that these scribes and Pharisees carry the authority of Moses, and their instructions are to be observed. But their conduct is not to be imitated since they don't practice what they preach. They have laid a heavy burden of ritual on others' shoulders and refused to lighten it, while their own pious practices are conducted wholly for display. They wear their ceremonial trappings ostentatiously. They revel in getting places of honor at supper parties and occupying important seats in the synagogue, in being greeted with deference in the marketplaces, and in being called 'Rabbi' and 'Master.'

"As for you, don't invite the title of 'Rabbi'; you have only one teacher and, among yourselves, only equality. Nor should you call anyone 'Father' on earth in the way you address your unique Father in heaven. And you should discourage others from calling you 'Master,' for your one and only 'Master' is the Messiah. Among you, the first must be last."

At this moment Jesus seems to have noticed some authorities at the edge of the crowd observing him narrowly. He took the opportunity to address them directly—very directly.

"You are courting disaster, you scribes, Pharisees, hypocrites! You bar others from the kingdom of God because you won't enter it yourselves. And you make prodigious efforts to convert an infidel, only to convert him into a devil more evil than yourselves!

"You are courting disaster, blind guides! You say that to make a vow in the name of the temple means nothing, but that a vow made in the name of the temple *gold* is binding! You say that a vow is binding if it is made in the name of the *gift* on the altar rather than in the name of the altar of God! You benighted idiots, is the gold holier than the temple, the gift holier than the altar? Can one swear by the temple and not by the gold, by the altar and not by the gift? Can one swear by heaven and not by God?

"You are courting disaster—scribes, Pharisees, hypocrites! You pay meticulous tithes on minims of condiments but neglect matters of substance under God's law—justice, mercy, faithfulness. You strain out a gnat before you drink, but then swallow a camel!

"You are courting disaster—scribes, Pharisees, hypocrites! You scrupulously clean the outside of your cups and bowls, while inside they are filled with avarice and luxury. Clean the inside, and the outside will take care of itself.

"You are courting disaster—scribes, Pharisees, hypocrites! You are like whitewashed tombs, outwardly presentable but inwardly full of rotting bones and noisome filth. You appear just before others, but within you are hypocritical and wicked. You honor the graves of the prophets and smugly congratulate yourselves because you think, had you been living then, you would not have participated in shedding their blood. Yet by your own testimony you are the heirs of the murderers. It is now time for you to complete their work.

"You serpents, spawn of vipers! How can you possibly escape the jaws of hell? You'll have your chance, as you'll see, for I'll be sending you prophets and sages, but you will scourge them, and hound them from town to town, and have them crucified. On your heads will rest the blame for the shedding of innocent blood, from that of Abel to that of Zachariah, whom your kind murdered in God's temple. The price will be paid by this generation."

Jesus paused for a moment, gazing sadly out beyond the temple walls. "O Jerusalem, Jerusalem," he exclaimed. "You have stoned and killed the very prophets sent to rescue you! How often I've yearned to protect your people, as a hen protects her chicks under her wing, but you have rejected me. You will see your houses deserted, but, I tell you, you will not see me again until I return and you greet me with the words, 'Blessed is he who comes in the name of the Lord.'"

He grew silent and seemed lost in thought. The authorities hurried away to make their wrathful reports, and gradually the crowd dispersed.

Needing some rest after such enervating rhetoric, Jesus sat down and idly watched the crowds milling about the treasury room, where people dropped money offerings for the temple into a collection box.

Those richly dressed, he noticed, dropped conspicuously generous amounts in with a flourish, but his eye was especially caught by a woman, dressed in threadbare widow's weeds, diffidently dropping two small copper coins into the box. Calling her to his disciples' attention, he observed, "While the others donated what they could easily afford, this poor woman gave all that she had. Her offering, I assure you, is worth more than all the rest put together."

Intimations of the Cross

Among the pilgrims visiting Jerusalem for the Passover feast were some interested but uncommitted Greeks. Since the Hebrew religion was a rather exclusive one, they may have been attracted by reports of Jesus' broader appeal to humanity in general, including those beyond the narrow pale of piety by writ and rote. They approached the apostle Philip, whose hometown of Bethsaida had a very Grecian flavor, and asked to meet Jesus. Philip agreed and, with his friend Andrew, brought them to him.

Jesus, delighted by this evidence that his message was attracting Gentile interest, addressed himself to their concern over exclusiveness, but rather incidentally. Evidently he found it significant that his message was spreading beyond the confines of Judaism, as though these Greeks had brought him the first inkling of the fulfillment of his mission and thus of the beginning of the end—an end that he dreaded but knew was inevitable.

"The time is finally at hand," he exclaimed, "for the Son of man to pass into his glory, just as a grain of wheat must die in the earth for wheat to live. *Any*one," he said, glancing at the Greeks, "who wants to may follow me and serve my cause wherever we may be, and thereby be honored by God."

As a crowd began to gather, Jesus turned to his disciples with a heavy sigh. "I'm deeply troubled," he said in a tone of mystical preoccupation. "Can I say, 'Father, spare me this ordeal'? How can I, when it's the reason for my being here? I must rather say, 'Father, may you glorify your name!'"

From the sky above a thunderous voice could be heard saying, "I have already glorified it, and will do so again." Or at least *something* was heard; some in the crowd said it was thunder, while others claimed it was an angel's voice. To Jesus it doubtless was a seal of approval on what he had done and would soon do. Although it surely strengthened his resolve, he was more concerned that it strengthen faith in his audience. "The voice you heard," he told them dryly, "spoke not for my sake but for yours."

"This world," he continued, "is now about to be judged, and its evil prince evicted. And I, raised upon a gibbet, will touch the hearts of all humanity."

A gibbet was not the sort of thing that Jews could readily associate with a conquering Messiah. Someone in the crowd— perhaps an agent of the authorities seeking to discredit Jesus—called out contentiously, "We are told by our Scriptures that the Messiah will stay with us forever. How can you say that the Son of man will be raised on a gibbet? If so, then who is this so-called Son of man?"

But Jesus was in no mood for frolicsome debate. Instead of answering his heckler, he simply repeated essentially something he had said before. "You'll have the light with you a little while longer. Take advantage of it, or you'll stumble along in the dark. Have faith in the light, and it will infuse your souls.

"If you hear my message but ignore it, that's not for me to judge now. I've come not to judge the world but to save it. Those who reject me and my message will be judged in the end by my teachings which come not from me but from my Father, who told me what to teach. And since I know that his instruction brings eternal life, I have taught as he instructed me."

And with that he left the scene to seek some rest in solitude.

An Apocalyptic Interlude [1]

The temple in Jerusalem was a wonder of the ancient world, and one day Jesus heard some of his disciples exclaiming over its magnificence. To counter their admiration of worldly splendor, he warned them again of the temple's total destruction, which, as Jews, they naturally equated with the final destruction of the world. When would this happen, some of them asked avidly, and what would be the portents of it? Jesus, less given to identifying the destruction of Jerusalem with that of the world, answered them at length but with mystical ambiguity. He didn't know the exact answer, nor was it part of his mission to provide such information.

"Be on your guard," he cautioned them, "against being led astray by those who assert, in my name, that they are the returned Christ. There'll be many of them, and they'll mislead many more. When wars and rumors of wars abound, don't be disturbed, for that doesn't mean the end is imminent. There will indeed be wars among nations, earthquakes, famines, epidemics of disease, and great celestial disturbances, but such things will be only the beginning.

"Before they occur, you will be hounded and persecuted, and in the hearts of many my message of love will grow cold. But in your response to this oppression the Holy Spirit will support you, and those who endure will be saved. My Good News must first be spread throughout the world; only then will the end come.

"As for Jerusalem, when you see her besieged by enemy armies, you will realize that her end has come. That will be the time for Judeans to flee the country, or to hide in the mountains, for those will be the days of disaster long prophesied. They will be days of special suffering for pregnant women and for women still nursing their infants. The city's people will be killed or dispersed in captivity, and the Gentile legions will trample the city down for as long as they please.

"At the end of the world, however, the sun and moon will grow dark, stars will fall from the sky, the sea will roar in turbulence, and

[1] By the time that the first century A.D. was entering its final quarter, Jerusalem had been demolished, the Christians' eager expectation of the world's end and the Second Coming was fading fast, and the Romans had begun persecuting the Christians in earnest. As a reflection of these times of trial, and in an effort to offer some hope of deliverance, an apocalyptic interlude was included in the slowly developing gospels. While it is wholly attributed to Jesus, some critics question how much of it comes from him.

people will faint with fear. Then will the Son of man come with his angels to gather together his faithful. So, when such things occur, lift up your eyes, for your redemption is at hand. Just as the budding of a fig tree heralds the summer, so these events will herald the kingdom of God. Yet just when it will arrive, only God the Father knows. Nevertheless, though the earth and the heavens perish, my message will endure.

"Always be ready for the coming of the Son of man, who may arrive when you least expect him. Be like the manager who does his work faithfully in the owner's absence, not like the manager who takes to drink and mistreats the workers—and whom the owner will discover and punish dreadfully. Be like the bridesmaids who filled their lamps with oil and were ready to light the way of the arriving bridegroom, not like the others who had to rush out to buy oil at the last minute and found the door closed to them on their return.

"When the Son of man comes, he will assign the sheep and the goats, the saved and the condemned, to places at his right and his left. And he'll say to those at his right, 'You are the ones blessed by my Father. Come now and claim your inheritance, the kingdom awaiting you since the beginning of the world. For you allayed my hunger, slaked my thirst, clothed me, sheltered me, and visited me in prison.' Then will they ask, 'When did we do such things for you?' And the Son of man will answer, 'Whatever you've done for any of my brothers or sisters, including the lowliest, you've done for me.'

"But to those at his left he'll say, 'Leave me, you cursed ones, for the everlasting fire prepared for Satan and his demons! For you refused to allay my hunger, slake my thirst, clothe me, shelter me, or visit me in prison.' Then will they ask, 'When did we refuse to do such things for you?' And he will answer, 'What you refused to do for the lowliest of my brothers and sisters, that you refused to do for me.'"

The Last Supper

As the time approached for celebration of the Passover, the authorities were in something of a quandary. They were very reluctant to leave Jesus free to stir up trouble during the festival; yet they hesitated to take any strong action against him lest it provoke a riot. At this point they received a visit which gave them an opportunity for a quick decision and immediate action before the festival began.

Their visitor was the apostle Judas Iscariot. What would they give him, he asked, to keep them apprised of Jesus' whereabouts so that they could arrest him quietly, away from any crowds? After a hurried consultation, they offered him thirty silver shekels (about three months' wages for a laborer), and he accepted.

Meanwhile, a couple of Jesus' disciples had gone into the city and, in accordance with some instructions from him, had reserved a large dining room in a private home and arranged for a supper to be prepared. When Jesus and the twelve apostles arrived late that afternoon, everything was ready. He was looking forward to sharing this supper with them, Jesus told the Twelve as he passed around a ceremonial cup of wine, for it would be his last before the coming of the kingdom of God.

Perhaps to forestall any distressing discussion of comparative rank in that kingdom, he removed his outer clothing, hung a towel at his waist, poured some water into a basin, and began washing his companions' road-dusty feet. Although this was normally a task for a servant, they seem to have accepted the situation with comfortable, if puzzled, equanimity. When he came to Peter, however, he ran into some resistance: "Lord, do *you* intend to wash *my* feet?"

"You may not understand this now," replied Jesus patiently, "but you will later."

Peter evidently was shocked at what he considered a reversal of proper roles, although, of course, he hadn't offered to wash anybody's feet. "You'll never wash *my* feet!" he remonstrated, pulling them away.

"If I don't," Jesus responded gently but adamantly, "our friendship's at an end."

"In that case," cried Peter the impulsive, thrusting his feet out again, "wash not only my feet, but my hands and head as well!" But Jesus assured him that only his feet needed washing, and they would suffice.

When he had finished and as he was putting his outer clothes back on, Jesus explained that he had merely tried to give them an example of rendering service to others regardless of rank, an example he hoped they would follow in many ways. But for one of them—the one who was about to betray him to the authorities—he continued as they began eating, he had no such hope.

The remark caused some consternation, with the apostles asking who among them could do such a thing, even inadvertently. As if in response, Jesus dipped a piece of bread into some sauce and handed it to Judas with an ironic suggestion, "What you aim to do, do quickly." But the significance of the gesture escaped the others, who assumed that the departing Judas was being sent on some prearranged errand in his capacity as treasurer for the group. In a sense, of course, he was.

Judas, willing agent of the inevitable, was to be the one person of whom Jesus said that it would be better for him if he'd never been born.

The supper continued in an atmosphere of muted conviviality. As it neared its end, Jesus called for everyone's undivided attention. In the ensuing hush he broke some bread, blessed it in ceremonial fashion with a prayer of thanks, and broke it into several pieces in a bowl. "Take this, my body," he said, holding out the bowl to be passed around, "and eat it."

After the bread had made the circuit, he took up a cup of wine, blessed it also with a prayer of thanks, and held it out to be passed around. "Drink, each of you," he asked them, "from this cup of my blood, the blood of the new testament, to be shed for the many, for forgiveness."

The apostles complied quietly with this mystical request. There was something oppressively ominous about this evening, and they were in anything but a boisterous mood. After ending the supper with a ceremonial hymn, they all left together for the Mount of Olives.

A Farewell Address

When they had climbed some distance up the hill, they stopped to rest in a lonely clearing. Jesus glanced around at his friends affectionately, evidently struck by their almost childlike vulnerability. "My children," he said with a sad smile, "I'll be with you now for only a little while longer. But I leave you a new commandment, that you love one another even as I have loved you. By showing such love, I hope, will you be recognized as my followers."

"But where are you going, Lord?" asked Peter anxiously.

"As I've said before," replied Jesus, "you can't follow me now to where I'm going, though one day you will do so."

"Why not now?" Peter persisted. "I'll willingly give up my life for you."

"Will you indeed?" sighed Jesus, with sorrow but no rancor. "I must warn you that before the cock crows to greet the morning, three times will you have disowned me."

Peter vigorously rejected this even as a possibility, and all the others similarly pledged their very lives. But Jesus merely shook his head dejectedly. Things wouldn't be the same, he told them, as when he sent disciples abroad without so much as traveling money because people would provide for them. Hostility would now replace such generosity, and they might be well advised to carry not only purses but also swords for their protection. Their immediate reaction—after a frantic search, they found that they had two swords among them—doubtless made him regret making the suggestion. In any case, he quickly changed the subject. Because he could sympathize with their growing apprehension from the depths of his own much sharper fear, he launched into a long discourse that emphasized the felicities of their long-term future over the miseries of their short-term prospects.

"Try not to be anxious," he said consolingly. "You trust God; trust me as well. I haven't misled you; there's plenty of room in my Father's house, and I must go to make things ready for you. When I return, I'll gather you all to me so that we'll be together. As for where I'm going"—he paused and then continued with a smile—"well, surely you know the way there."

Thomas was never one to pretend to knowledge that he didn't have. "No, Lord," he protested. "We've no idea where you're going, so how could we know the way?"

As he so often did, Jesus addressed his answer to that aspect of the question that he considered important. "*I* am the way," he replied firmly. "I am the truth, and I am life itself. No one reaches the Father except through me. If you had understood me better, you would have perceived the Father, as you will before long."

"Reveal the Father to us, Lord," Philip interrupted, grasping at the straw. "The vision will be enough to sustain us."

"Oh, Philip," sighed Jesus. "We've been together all this time, and you still don't recognize me? Whoever really sees me sees the Father, yet you ask me to reveal him to you? Believe me, I am within the Father as he is within me. Believe this if only because of the marvelous things you've seen done. Such things, and my message as well, come not simply from me but from my Father within me.

"In my absence, I predict, you who believe in me will do such things, and even more marvelous things, in my name. I'll do anything you ask if the Son can thereby honor the Father.

"As you love me, obey my commandments. At my request the Father will send you another Intercessor to remain with you always—the very Spirit of truth, whom the worldly will reject but whom you'll receive in your inmost hearts. I'll never abandon you.

"Soon the worldly will no longer see me, but you'll see me; as I live, so will you. Then will you realize that I live in my Father, that you live within me and I within you. Those who keep my commandments are the ones who love me and are loved by my Father and me, and to whom I'll reveal myself."

"But, Lord," asked one of the apostles, "how is it that you'll reveal yourself to us but not to the worldly?"

"Only those who already love me and live by my message," answered Jesus, "will welcome my Father and me. Those who don't love me will ignore my message, though, in truth, it comes from the Father himself.

"I've preached that message to you for as long as we've been together. After me the Holy Spirit, the Intercessor sent from the Father, will teach you and remind you of all I've told you. I leave my peace with you—not worldly satisfaction, but my inward peace. So banish fear from your hearts. You've heard me say that I must leave you but will return. Your love for me should have made you rejoice that I'm going to the Father, because he is greater than I. But your faith isn't strong enough; indeed, I've told you about these events beforehand so that, when they come about, your faith will be strengthened.

"I haven't much longer to talk with you. The evil prince of this world is approaching. Although he can't overcome me, I must submit as ordered, so that all may see the love I bear for the Father."

The sight of a nearby grapevine lured him into allegory. "I am the vine of truth, and my Father is the caretaker. He cuts off the dead branches and prunes the others to make them more fruitful. I am the vine, you are the branches. As the branch must take its life from the vine to bear fruit, so must you take your life from me. Without that life, a branch grows dry and is destroyed. But with that life, you, my disciples, will bear much fruit and thereby honor my Father. Live by my message and you'll live in my love, just as I live by my Father's bidding and live in his love. I tell you this to fill you with my joy and happiness.

"Love one another as I love you; no one can show greater love than to give up his life for his friends. You *are* my friends, you know, not my servants, for I've passed on to you what my Father has entrusted to me. You didn't choose me; I chose you, as branches prepared to bear lasting fruit. I have appointed you, and so whatever you ask in my Father's name, it will be yours.

"So love one another. If the worldly treat you with malice, remember how they treated me. They love their own kind, not your kind, which is the kind I chose. As I've said before, a follower is no less vulnerable than the leader; if they persecute me, they'll persecute you, too. However, those who would accept my message from me will accept it from you as well. What you will suffer at their hands will be on my account, since they refuse to acknowledge the one who sent me here. If I hadn't given them the message, they would have been innocent enough; as it is, however, they have no excuse. But they are fulfilling a passage in their Scripture, that they have hated me without reason.

"I tell you this, about our sharing their mistreatment, lest you be disillusioned. They'll throw you out of their synagogues, and the time will come when putting you to death will be considered a service to God, since they recognize neither him nor me. When such things happen, you may remember that I forewarned you; not at the outset did I warn you, but now that I must leave you I am warning you."

Pausing, he expectantly swept their worried faces with his eyes, but they remained silent. "This time no one asks where I'm going," he commented. Then he continued more sympathetically, "The news of my leaving has saddened you. Yet I assure you, it's better for you that I leave so that I can send you the Intercessor who will show up the guilt of the worldly in their rejection of me, in their pious righteousness (for I who condemned it will be vindicated, abiding in heaven with the Father), and in their condemnation of me (for their prince of evil will have fallen in defeat).

"I have much more to tell you, but it would be too much now for you to absorb. The Spirit of truth, however, will guide you in the meaning of my message, on questions of the present and the future, and this will do me the honor of promulgating my message intact. And so, as I've said, soon you'll see me no longer, but then later you'll see me again."

Since at least some of the apostles still hadn't a glimmer of what he was talking about—given the mystical difficulties of the subject, it was not entirely their fault nor his—he tried to offer them further reassurance that their travail wouldn't last forever. "Does this talk of going and coming puzzle you?" he asked. "The main thing is that soon you will be mourning, while the worldly rejoice, but your sorrow will be turned into joy, like the joy of a proud new mother who no longer remembers the pain of her labor. Your sorrow will be transformed by my return into a joy that no one can take from you, and you'll no longer be puzzled. As for what you wish from my Father—ask in my name, and you'll find joy indeed in his response.

"I've spoken to you a great deal in metaphor, but the time is coming when I'll tell you about the Father much more plainly. Then will you make your requests in my name, and I'll not have to make them to the Father for you, because he loves you for loving me and believing that he sent me. From him I came into the world, and to him I now go from the world."

"Why, you're speaking plainly enough now!" exclaimed one of the apostles, amid much nodding in agreement. Then, perhaps because they felt that Jesus had read their thoughts, he added, "Now we recognize that you know everything, including unasked questions. This shows us that you, indeed, have come from God."

Jesus was evidently not deeply impressed by this sudden turn. "So now you really believe me?" he countered skeptically. "I tell you, the time is almost here when you will be scattered and will leave me deserted, except for my Father's presence. Nevertheless, I've told you all this to reassure you: however this world mistreats you, take heart, for I have transcended it."

Perhaps he found their general reaction to his reassurances less than reassuring. Whatever the reason, Jesus now turned to someone more dependable. Growing thoughtful, he lifted his eyes in prayer. "Father, the hour has come. Grant honor to your Son, that your Son may bring honor to you. You have given him dominion over all humanity to bring eternal life to those you've entrusted to him, so that they may thereby acknowledge you as the one true God, and me as your emissary.

"I have glorified you here on earth by fulfilling the mission that you gave me; now grant me the glory of your presence such as I possessed before the beginning of the world. I have revealed you to those whom you designated, and they have accepted your message. They know now that the message comes from you as I delivered it, that I am indeed your messenger.

"I pray for them—not for the world at large, but for those whom you put in my care. They belong to you, but, as all things mine are yours and yours are mine, they do me honor.

"I have little time left now in this world, but they will remain when I leave. Holy Father, as you entrusted them to me, now keep them true to you, in loving unity even as you and I. While in their company, I've kept them true and protected them, and not one has been lost—except the outlaw who now fulfills the prophecy from Scripture. Before I return to you, I ask these things so that my joy may fill them to the brim.

"I have brought them your message, but the worldly have despised them, for they are no more worldly than I am. I ask that you protect them not from the world but from the evil in it. Dedicate them to truth, the truth of your message, for as you sent me to inform the world, so will I send them now. May my dedication be theirs.

"I pray, too, Father, for those who believe in me on their testimony, that all may be as one as you and I are one, that all the world may accept me as your messenger, that the unity of all believers may be so perfect that all the world may recognize your love.

"Father, I ask that those in my care may be at my side to see my glory, the glory of your love for me from before the beginning of the world. The world fails to recognize you, but I know you, and these followers of mine have received me as your messenger. I have revealed you to them, and I will reveal you through them. May your love for me live on within them. And so may I."

Gethsemane

On the Mount of Olives there was a large orchard of olive trees called Gethsemane (Aramaic for "oil press"). When Jesus and his companions arrived there, he asked them to sit and wait while he went farther into the orchard to pray. Taking Peter, James, and John with him, he walked on in a state of growing agitation.

Anyone who has ever dreaded surgery—and especially anyone also acquainted with the cunning cruelties of crucifixion—can begin to imagine what he was going through. The next eighteen hours or so were to bring him as much agony of body and soul as perhaps anyone can bear. Although this was a common fate for deviants under Roman law, that fact made the experience no less dreadful for the individual.

"I am deathly ill with fear and anguish," he confided softly to the three apostles. "Wait here," he said. And then pathetically, as though reaching out desperately for human company in his lonely terror, he added, "And stay awake with me." While they settled down on the ground, leaning against a tree, he went a short distance away and, kneeling down unsteadily, lost himself in prayer.

"My Father, Almighty One," he begged, "if possible, spare me this cup of suffering." He paused. As he realized the futility of this appeal, the dishonor in evading his role as scapegoat, he broke into a bloody sweat of stinging fear. Then with a prodigious effort he stiffened his resolve and added, "Yet it's not my will, Father, but yours that must be done." As if in response to these words of selfless obedience, he had a vision of an angel beside him, offering support and encouragement.

When he was able, he rose and returned to the three apostles, only to find them sound asleep. Waking them, he asked Peter sadly, "Couldn't you stay awake with me for a single hour? Try to keep awake now, and pray to resist temptation." Then, perhaps softened by Peter's look of guilty embarrassment, he said, "Your spirit is willing enough, but your body is weak."

He peered through the trees expectantly. He was waiting now, while time dragged on excruciatingly. Again he withdrew and prayed for relief; again he returned to find the three asleep, and even once again. The third time, however, he told them to get up and follow him toward the source of some commotion that had arisen in the orchard. "My betrayer," he explained, "has finally arrived."

Indeed, he had. Through the trees came the minions of authority: Judas and an impressive throng of temple police and assorted thrill seekers, equipped with swords, clubs, and torches, the last casting a flickering, ghostly glow over the proceedings. Judas, who had told the police that he would identify Jesus for them by a kiss of greeting, did just that with a great show of loving respect. "O Judas!" Jesus murmured to him in response, "Do you now betray the Son of man with a kiss?"

As the police seized Jesus and began to lead him away, Peter impulsively grabbed a sword and swung it at the head of a policeman, slashing his ear. For a moment the commotion ceased; everyone was silent with shock. It was a tense moment, but Jesus quickly relieved the tension. "No, no," he cried, freeing himself and stepping back, "put away that sword; use it, and it will bring you death." Then, reaching out to the wounded man, he touched his ear and healed it.

"And you," he added sardonically, turning to the crowd, "why have you come out here armed like this, as though to catch a robber? I spent day after day with you in the temple, and you didn't raise a hand against me." He paused and sighed. "But now get on with it. The prophecies must be fulfilled, and I must drink from the cup as my Father commands."

Again they seized him and led him away, this time without interruption. As he had predicted, his friends eluded the police and left without ceremony. One was so eager to get away that he left his cloak behind in the unfriendly grasp of a policeman, fleeing into the night without a stitch.

Trial by Ordeal

The Judean high priesthood in the early part of the first century seems to have been something of a family affair. At about the time of Jesus' birth, the patriarch of the clan, Annas, had been high priest. Since he had been succeeded in the post by four sons and a son-in-law, the present high priest Caiaphas, the extent of his influence can well be imagined. Part of Jesus' unhappy fate was to have this formidable cabal arrayed against him.

And so it was that he found himself, a bound captive, led to the residence of Annas for questioning. He proved to be an uncooperative witness, refusing to answer Annas' questions about his "organization" and his religious opinions—perhaps partly because, under Jewish law, he wasn't required to testify against himself. "I've preached to the people quite openly," he asserted, "in the synagogues, in the temple, before large gatherings—never in secret. So why ask *me*? Ask rather those who have heard me; they can report what I said."

His lack of servility before this pretentious pooh-bah so shocked an officer of his guard that the man cuffed Jesus, exclaiming, "Is this the way you answer a high priest?"

"If I've said something wicked," countered Jesus, "then present the evidence. If not, why did you strike me?"

Possibly Annas was getting too old to handle anything but obsequious confessions, especially in the small hours of the morning. Abruptly adjourning the hearing, he sent Jesus on to Caiaphas, who was already conducting a similarly irregular inquisition.

By the time Jesus and his guards arrived, the high priest and some other council members had already collected a number of people to testify against Jesus. Their testimony proved so vague and contradictory, however—especially about destroying the temple and raising it again in three days—that the proceedings quickly took on a tinge of purple frustration. Finally Caiaphas turned on Jesus and asked, rather shrilly, "Haven't you any answer to the charges these people are making against you?" But Jesus simply stared at him without a word.

"Well, then," Caiaphas asked him, gambling on an incriminating response, "are you the anointed Messiah, Son of the Holy One?"

"That I am," replied Jesus evenly. "Furthermore, you will yet see this Son of man sitting with honor by the side of the Almighty, approaching amid the clouds of heaven."

Although technically this mystical assertion may not have been blasphemy under Jewish law, it was close enough to provoke Caiaphas into tearing his clothes (a ritual reaction to blasphemy) and exclaiming, "What do we need witnesses for? You've heard this blasphemy! What's your verdict?"

The rump council's opinion was unanimous: the culprit deserves the death penalty. Since the hearing was unofficial—being more in the nature of an impetuous kangaroo court—the verdict also was unofficial. But it would suffice, the authorities hoped, to persuade the Roman governor to do his duty, or at least their bidding.

Their decision allowed Jesus' guards thereupon to engage in a round of vicious fun. They pummeled their helpless victim. They spit in his face. Blindfolding him, they taunted him, "Show us your prophetic vision, Messiah; tell us who struck you." And so on. To the tender mercies of such as these was their Savior now entrusted.

While this was going on, Peter was standing just outside, making himself as inconspicuous as possible beside a small group of temple police, warming his hands with them by a fire. With a little craning, now and then he could get a glimpse of Jesus through one of the portals. As he stood there, a servant woman passed by, gave him a searching glance, and muttered, "Why, you were one of those with the Nazarene, this Jesus."

Peter, with a show of indignant innocence, protested, "I don't know what you're talking about!" The woman shrugged and went on her way. Since the police, absorbed in their own conversation, had taken no notice, Peter decided to stay.

In a little while, however, another woman came by and made the same remark. Peter made a similar response, this time accompanied by an oath, "I tell you, I don't know the man!" Evidently attracted by the vehemence of his denial, several people now entered into the conversation with remarks like "You *must* be one of his company; your Galilean accent gives you away!" Peter, now totally absorbed in his efforts at dissociation, began to embroider his denials with a great deal of heartfelt profanity. But in the middle of a curse, he caught sight of Jesus looking directly at him, silently but eloquently. The look silenced him instantly, and at that moment he heard a cock crow in the distance.

The police were staring at him suspiciously but made no move. They probably had no direct orders to round up Jesus' followers and, just as probably, were reluctant to leave the warm glow of the fire. Peter, gathering his cloak about him, hurried away until he came to a deserted spot, where he leaned weakly against a pillar and wept bitter, bitter tears.

But he did not despair. In contrast, Judas, according to one report, "went out and hanged himself."

The Long Arm of Rome

Early the next morning—after a night in which, we can presume, Jesus was given little or no rest—the temple police took their prisoner to the Jerusalem residence of Pontius Pilate. A party of authorities, chiefly priests, and an attendant claque followed in their footsteps, for this was to be a public trial, however hastily arranged.

In all likelihood Pilate was thoroughly chagrined to have this controversy laid, almost literally, at his doorstep. Although he despised the Jewish culture, he could be intimidated by the Jewish authorities, who had embarrassed him more than once by appealing directly to Tiberius Caesar. The emperor was a hard-nosed autocrat who could be very severe with provincial governors for interfering in a colony's internal affairs but who, conversely and perhaps perversely, could grow downright paranoid at any hint of treason or rebellion in a colony or elsewhere. Pilate must have known already that the official hostility against Jesus arose from some obscure internal conflict; yet he could never countenance anything resembling treason. He must have considered the affair trivial and thoroughly ridiculous, yet fraught with danger to his precious career.

When Jesus was brought before him in the hearing room, he asked the Jewish authorities to state the charges. They first answered that this upstart had been undermining the Jewish nation. When Pilate seemed quite unmoved by this, they offered two additional, and more imaginative, charges in the hope of exciting his interest. The fellow had denounced the paying of Roman taxes, they piously complained, and had called himself a king.

On hearing this, Pilate took Jesus into an adjoining room for private questioning. "*Are* you the king of the Jews?" he asked with a touch of anxiety.

Jesus was in no condition to debate notions of kingship with someone of totally different philosophy, but he summoned up enough strength to reply with a pointed question: "Do you ask this because you want to know the answer or because some others have already given you an answer?"

Pilate was not about to be associated in anyone's mind with those he considered to be fanatic barbarians. "Am I a Jew?" he retorted irritably. "Your own authorities have brought you here. What have you done?"

Jesus replied with an answer of sorts to both his questions. "My kingdom isn't part of this world. If it were, my followers would have fought against my being taken."

"Well, *are* you a king, then," asked Pilate in matter-of-fact Roman style, "or aren't you?"

"The word 'king' is your word," answered Jesus. "I was born into this world for one purpose only, to bring news of the truth. Anyone who can recognize the truth will hear it in my message."

"The *truth*?" snorted the Roman. "What *is* the truth?"

Convinced for the moment that Jesus was a dreamer, a mystic about as dangerous to the empire as a lamb in a den of wolves, Pilate left the room and informed the Jewish authorities and assorted retinue that he could find nothing criminal in the man. During the tumult of protest that followed this announcement, he learned (or was reminded) that Jesus was a Galilean. Since this meant that Herod might have jurisdiction in the case and since Herod happened to be in town for the festival, Pilate seized the opportunity to pack Jesus and his accusers off to Herod, surely in the hope that he'd never have to see any of them again.

The ploy proved unsuccessful. Although Herod may have been pleased by Pilate's ostensible courtesy and hopeful that he could satisfy some of his curiosity about Jesus' wonder-working, he found Jesus totally uncooperative—adamantly silent, in fact, while the priests' frenzied charges swirled about him. In retaliation, Herod ordered some soldiers of his guard to taunt and bedevil the prisoner and to send him back to Pilate bedecked in humiliating outer finery. According to the Gospel of Luke, this episode improved relations between Herod and Pilate, although the latter can hardly have been delighted to see the problem back on his doorstep.

Grasping at any and every opportunity, the governor informed the Jewish prosecutors that Herod's reaction was further evidence of Jesus' innocence. Since he was about to grant the customary amnesty to some Jewish prisoner in honor of the festival, he argued, it might as well be Jesus, mightn't it?

"No, no," shouted the priests and their well-trained claque, "give us Barabbas!" Barabbas was a popular anti-Roman who was then in jail, evidently for insurrection, robbery, and murder.

"What, then, shall I do about this fellow you call the King of the Jews?" asked Pilate in a voice sharp with contempt.

The answer came in repeated shouts, "Crucify him!"

"Why?" barked Pilate. "What crime has he committed?"

The crowd ignored this irrelevancy. "Crucify him! Crucify him!"

Pilate was in a torment of indecision. He had earlier received a report from his wife of a dream she had had warning against any punishment of this innocent prisoner. As a practical, godless man in a world of uncertainty, he was quite vulnerable to superstition. In his desperation he now did something that no self-respecting governor would ever have done in any ordinary circumstances: he called for a basin of water and washed his hands in public to signify his refusal to take any responsibility in the affair. It was, of course, one of history's most futile gestures.

He had one more delaying tactic. He turned Jesus over to some soldiers of his guard, evidently taking a page from Herod's book and then embroidering it. After a severe whipping, the soldiers placed a cloak of royal purple about their victim's shoulders and a roughly woven crown of thorny tendrils on his head; and, for a final touch, they thrust a long reed to serve as a scepter into the bonds about his wrists. Pilate then had him brought out, thus arrayed, before his accusers, apparently in the hope that his humiliation might appease their fury and that his pitiable condition might soften their obstinacy.

"Look at the poor fellow!" he exclaimed. "I want you to know that I find him guiltless."

But again the shouts arose, "Crucify him!"

"Then *you* crucify him!" retorted Pilate. "I know of no crime that he's committed." He had to know that they had no legal authority to crucify anyone, but then he was very upset.

"He has broken our law," cried one of the priests, "by claiming to be the Son of God."

Unnerved by this retort, since divinity was the province of Roman emperors, Pilate again withdrew with Jesus for some private questioning. "Where *do* you come from?" he asked nervously. But Jesus simply stared at him in silence.

"What? You won't answer?" exclaimed Pilate angrily. "Don't you realize that I have the power to set you free or have you crucified?"

"You haven't any power over me," Jesus retorted, "except whatever is granted to you from above. You are only less guilty than the people who turned me over to you."

Dismayed by this enigmatic but ominous remark, Pilate again led Jesus out and asked his accusers what he hoped they would take as a rhetorical question, "This is your king! Am I to crucify your king?"

"To the cross with him!" came a shout, frenzied but cunning. "We have no king but Caesar!"

The implications were clear, and they ended Pilate's irresolution. He turned Jesus over to his soldiers with instructions for his crucifixion.

The Cross

Relieved of the purple cloak and dressed once more in his own clothing, Jesus, growing ever weaker with fatigue and suffering, was led out of the Roman headquarters with a crossbeam slung across his shoulders. His destination was perhaps four or five hundred yards away, a mound called Golgotha ("Skull Hill," reputedly because of its shape) just outside the inner city walls. Somewhere along the route he proved too exhausted to carry the beam any farther, at which point the Roman squad in charge dragooned a strapping fellow named Simon into carrying it the rest of the way.

The people that lined the street were subdued, and most seemed distressed in varying degrees. A number of women grieved openly at the sight of Jesus' suffering, although he reportedly managed to stop long enough to warn them that they might more fittingly grieve over the ultimate fate of their children and their city.

At the execution site, Jesus, after being offered an anesthetic drink and refusing it, was crucified—probably with nails through his wrists, fixing his outspread arms to the crossbeam, and through his feet, attaching them to the bottom of the post on which the crossbeam was mounted and secured. The soldiers then fastened a sign to the crossbeam, rising above Jesus' head and revealing his crime with a sardonic Roman inscription in Aramaic, Latin, and Greek: JESUS, KING OF THE JEWS. (Some Jewish authorities went to Pilate about this, demanding that the inscription be edited to read, *"He said,* 'I am King of the Jews,'" but the exasperated Pilate flatly refused, reportedly exclaiming, "What I have written, I have written!")

Crucifixion is a death by several kinds of torture, including public humiliation, excruciating pain, intense thirst, muscle cramps, shock, heart failure, suffocation; it is a slow death, lasting for periods of from several hours to several days, depending on the particular methods used and the prior condition of the victim. The ordeal seems to have lasted, on the average, about twelve hours; the crucifixion of Jesus, who was already weak from his previous ordeals, lasted about six, from midmorning to midafternoon.

As the soldiers surveyed their completed work, the pinioned Jesus gazed at them and, with painful breath, murmured a prayer in a simple distillation of his message: "Father, forgive them; they don't know what they're doing." As he said it, they began dividing his few clothes—the only spoils available—among them and gambling for his cloak and, in the process, fulfilling a prophecy contained in a scriptural psalm.

On each side of Jesus stood another cross holding a convicted criminal, but apparently it was Jesus who drew the crowds. Clusters of his adversaries especially were in evidence, mocking him with gestures and with cries, such as "You who were going to destroy the temple and restore it in three days, rescue yourself now. If you're the Son of God, step down from the cross!" A number of priests and other authorities, also in eager attendance, joined in with their own contributions, such as "He was so good at saving others, and now he can't save himself!" and "Why, he's King of the Jews—just step down from the cross, and we'll believe it." Even one of the criminals began flinging taunts from his cross until he was stopped by the other, who had strength enough to shout back, "We deserve what we're getting, but this fellow's innocent!" Then he murmured to Jesus, "Remember me, Jesus, when you attain your kingdom."

"I assure you," Jesus responded weakly, "you'll find happiness with me this very day."

In the crowd shuffling about before him he could find no friendly face. Loneliness and a sense of abandonment now were added to his burdens. After a while, however, he saw his mother and her sister standing nearby with Mary Magdalene and the apostle John. The sight of his mother must have wrenched his heart, powerless as he was to comfort her. With an effort, he looked at her and then at John, saying to them as best he could, "Mother, there is your son," and "Son, there is your mother." And, indeed, John took her home with him that day and cared for her.

Toward midafternoon, as the sky grew dark with an approaching storm, Jesus suffered a paroxysm, audibly crying out, "My God, my God, why have you abandoned me?" Because this cry of lonely agony was in Aramaic, a man in the crowd mistook the phrase "My God" ("Eloi" or "Eli") for a call upon the prophet Elias. Impaling a sponge on the end of a stick, he soaked it in the sour wine kept for the soldiers and held it up to Jesus' mouth, evidently in an effort to lessen his thirst and perhaps revive him. But others in the crowd called to him, "Hold off! Let's see whether Elias will come to rescue him!"

With the shock of feeling the wine-soaked sponge against his face, however, Jesus, recoiling with an agonizing effort, muttered, "Now is it accomplished!" Then, after calling out in a louder voice, "Father, to you I entrust my spirit," he slumped forward and died.

The Tomb

The reports of the events immediately following Jesus' death vary greatly. This may be due partly to the consternation and confusion among the few disciples still at the scene and partly to some symbolic embellishment of the reports when they came to be written down a generation later. Evidently the storm grew much worse, with wind gusts strong enough to rip apart the curtain that protected the Holy of Holies in the temple. One Gospel (Matthew) reports an earthquake that cracked open a number of graves, adding a gothic detail to the effect that bodies emerged from the grave and were later encountered in the city.

The reports agree, however, that the Roman soldiers were much impressed either by the storm or by the dignity of Jesus' death or both, their captain going so far as to stare at Jesus' limp body and exclaim that this was, indeed, a godly man. While some of Jesus' friends waited some distance away—the women are especially mentioned—the soldiers made sure that the three crucified victims were dead so that the bodies, in line with Jewish regulations, could be removed before the start of the Sabbath at sunset. Because the two men flanking Jesus weren't clearly dead, the soldiers broke their legs. Incredibly, this was something of an act of mercy, since hanging by the arms alone could be expected to bring on almost immediate suffocation. Jesus, however, was so obviously dead that one of the soldiers merely pierced his side with a lance, drawing a mixture of blood and water (presumably lung fluids). To those disciples acquainted with Scripture and fond of symbolism, this was significant; the book of Exodus carries a prohibition against breaking the bones of the lamb sacrificed for the Passover.

It was late afternoon now, and time was running short, but a man of action appeared on the scene. Joseph, a resident of a town called Arimathea and a man of wealth and status—and a secret follower of Jesus—had courageously gone to Pilate with a request that he be allowed to take care of Jesus' body. Pilate, after checking with the captain of the guard to make sure that Jesus was, indeed, dead, granted the request. Joseph, with the help of Nicodemus, then moved the body from the cross to a cave which he had recently ordered outfitted as a tomb. After wrapping the body, together with a large quantity of scented embalming ointments, in a linen sheet, the two men laid it in the tomb, rolled the large closure stone across the entrance, and departed as inconspicuously as possible, unknowingly leaving behind them Mary Magdalene and another woman, who had followed them to make sure of the tomb's location.

The next morning a delegation of priests and Pharisees visited Pilate to remind him that "that imposter" had said something about rising from the dead on the third day, and to ask that the tomb be secured with a guard until after that time. Jesus' disciples, they explained to the half-listening Pilate, could steal the body and then claim that he had risen, and this final imposture could vindicate all the impostures that Jesus had committed while alive.

Pilate, eager to be rid of the whole affair, let them have a guard but told them otherwise to take care of the matter themselves. This they did, closing the tomb with a seal of some sort and posting a guard over it.

Victory 8

Although the priests and Pharisees apparently felt free to conduct business of sorts on the Sabbath day following Jesus' death, his disciples did not. So it wasn't until the morning after the Sabbath, at dawn, that Mary Magdalene and a few other women arrived back at the tomb with burial spices, presumably unaware of what Joseph and Nicodemus had done after disappearing into the tomb with the body. Doubtless the women were nourishing a faint hope that they wouldn't be turned away by the guard.

Their solicitous preparations, however, proved unnecessary. Upon approaching the tomb, they found the guards lying comatose at the entrance, the huge stone rolled to one side, and an angelic young person clothed in dazzling white sitting inside. The crucified Jesus, they were informed, was no longer there but had risen and would meet his disciples in Galilee. The frightened women fled back to the other disciples without a word to anyone else and breathlessly gave them the news.

The other disciples, faithful to the male chauvinism of their times, at first dismissed the report as an hysterical fancy. Peter and John, nevertheless, after some sober second thoughts, ran to the tomb to investigate. In the otherwise empty tomb, now deserted by guards and angels alike, they found the burial linens lying undisturbed. Although this meant to them that the body could not have been stolen, no other explanation occurred to them. And so they returned to their friends with puzzled frowns and very puzzling news.

Mary Magdalene, who had followed the two men but hadn't

entered the tomb, now stayed behind, keeping a mournful vigil for the only man, in all likelihood, who had ever treated her as a person. She stood there for some time, weeping and occasionally peering wistfully into the tomb. After a while she thought she saw two angelic forms inside the cave and heard one of them ask, "Mistress, why are you weeping?"

"Because they have taken my Lord away," she replied sadly and somewhat fearfully, "and I have no idea where."

As she slowly turned to leave, she became aware of a man standing nearby. Why was she weeping, he asked her, and for whom was she looking?

Assuming that he was the caretaker, she replied, "Sir, if it was you who removed him, tell me where you've taken him, so that I can go and get him."

The man's response, a single word, must have been spoken with deep affection: "Mary."

Recognizing Jesus' voice immediately, she joyfully cried out, "Rabbi!" Flinging herself down before him, she grasped his feet lightly with trembling hands.

"No, Mary," he protested gently. "You mustn't hold on to me so, for I haven't yet gone to my Father. Go back to my friends, and tell them that I'm going to my Father—and the Father of all of you as well—to my God and yours."

And so, with tears of joy now, Mary returned to the other disciples to tell them that she had seen the Lord and to give them his message.

Meanwhile, the soldiers of the guard had returned to render a sheepish report to the priests at the temple. After a hurried conference, the priests gave them some money and instructed them to say that the body had been stolen; they would see to it that Pilate would be given no reason to punish them for negligence. The soldiers, delighted to comply, spread the story far and wide.

Keeping Up Appearances

Later that day, two of Jesus' disciples were walking along the road to Emmaus, a village a few miles northwest of Jerusalem, both of them totally absorbed in discussing the events of the past three days. In their preoccupation they failed to notice a man walking rapidly behind them until he overtook them and asked if he could join them. They readily agreed.

"What have you two been talking about so earnestly?" asked Jesus whom, for whatever reason, they failed to recognize.

The question halted them in their tracks. They stared at him in sad amazement. "Are you the only visitor to Jerusalem," asked one of them, named Cleophas, "who doesn't know what's been happening there these past few days?"

"Happening?" asked Jesus in an elaborate display of country-bumpkin ignorance. "What's been happening?"

"Why, this affair of Jesus of Nazareth," replied Cleophas as they resumed walking. Since this listener showed continued ignorance but some curiosity, he went on. "He said and did things that were wonderful in the eyes of God and the people, but our chief priests and other authorities turned him over to the Romans to be condemned and crucified."

After a moment's pause, he continued wistfully, "We'd hoped that he was the one destined to restore all Israel, but it's already been three days since he died. In fact, some of the women in our group went to his tomb and came back saying that they couldn't find his body but had a vision of angels who told them that he was, er, still alive. Then a couple of the men went to the tomb, but they couldn't find Jesus either."

"How slow you all are," exclaimed Jesus, "in believing what the prophets predicted! Wasn't the Messiah destined for that very ordeal to achieve his glory?" Since they responded with puzzled frowns, he launched into an explanation of the Scriptures related to the Messiah and his mission. And since they seemed fascinated, he continued until they were on the outskirts of Emmaus, where he began to say good-bye. But they pointed out how late it was getting to be and prevailed on him to be their overnight guest.

He accepted their invitation but not, as it turned out, to stay the night. During supper he took up a large piece of bread, blessed it, broke it into several pieces, and gave some to each of them. It was a process so much like the one they had heard about that they suddenly recognized him, and, quite as suddenly, he disappeared. They could hardly contain their chagrin. "Didn't he set our hearts on fire," asked one in both excitement and disappointment, "with his expounding of the Scriptures?"

And so they rushed back to Jerusalem, searched out the apostles—who, in their growing apprehension, were now huddled together in a room to which no invitations were being issued—and eagerly reported their experience. The apostles, though courteously receptive to their news, seemed less impressed than the two men had anticipated because, they learned to their further chagrin, Jesus had already appeared to Peter.

Late that evening, while the disciples were discussing their various experiences and reactions (only the apostle Thomas was absent), Jesus, despite the locked doors, unexpectedly appeared among them, giving several the fright of their lives, since they were sure they were seeing a ghost.

"Peace to you all," he said with a smile. "Why are you so fearful? Why do you have such anxious thoughts? Here, look at my hands and my feet; it is I, none other. No ghost has such flesh and bones as you see here." But, although he showed them the wounds in his hands and feet, they held back, partly out of fear that all this was too good to believe.

"Have you anything to eat?" he asked, glancing about casually.

Someone handed him a bit of broiled fish, and someone else a piece of honeycomb, and to everyone's delight he ate some of both. With this their disbelief began to melt, and soon they were crowding about him happily and listening to him more attentively than they ever had before.

Among other things, he took the occasion to suggest that his mission now had become their mission: "As the Father commissioned me, so do I now commission you." In fact, he went further, breathing on them symbolically (a root meaning of "spirit" is "breath") and adding, "Accept the Holy Spirit; the sins that you forgive will be forgiven, but those you won't forgive, they will remain."

Some time after he had left, Thomas arrived and was excitedly informed of Jesus' appearance. Aware that they had all been living in a state of anxiety and desperate hope, he evidently dismissed their experience as an understandable case of wishful hallucination. "See here," he finally responded to their persistent assurances, "unless I can see and touch the wounds from the nails in his hands and feet, and the wound from the lance in his side, I won't believe a word you've told me."

He was as good as *his* word; a week later he was with the others in the same circumstances—the same room with doors securely locked—and was still holding tight to his cynical view when Jesus materialized in their midst with the same greeting, "Peace to you all."

He looked at Thomas with an irrepressible twinkle. "And now, Thomas," he said, "look at my hands, and feel the wounds, and the wound in my side as well. Play the cynic no longer; have some faith in me."

As so often happens with cynics, Thomas did an about-face on the spot. "My Lord and my God!" he cried, bowing his head in acknowledgment.

"You believe in me now because you've seen me," smiled Jesus. "God will bless those others who don't see me but who believe in me nevertheless."

And then, presumably, he left as unexpectedly and mysteriously as he had come.

Some considerable time later, after the disciples had returned to Galilee, Peter and half a dozen others went out on the lake to try their luck at fishing. Their luck was miserable; they went out in the evening, but when dawn broke, they had yet to catch a single fish of any commercial value.

In the dawn's early light they could make out a man standing on the beach, watching them as they worked away about a hundred yards offshore. "Well, boys," he called to them, "do you have any fish?"

"Not a one," one or two of them called back wearily.

"Then try the right side of your boat," the man shouted. "Go ahead; throw out the net."

Desperate, willing to try anything, they did as he suggested. To their astonishment, the net became so heavy with fish that they couldn't lift it into the boat. The apostle John, dimly recalling a similar incident, nudged Peter excitedly, "It's the Lord!"

Peter, his memory jogged, impetuously grabbed his tunic, tucked it under his belt, jumped out of the boat into the shallow water, and began wading to shore, followed by the others as they struggled to maneuver the boat and the half-immersed net of fish in the right direction.

When they finally reached the shore, they found Jesus and Peter waiting for them beside a newly started fire and, ironically, a plentiful breakfast of broiled fish and toasted bread. At Jesus' suggestion, they hauled the straining net on shore and counted their catch which amounted to 153 fish. (The record is so unaccountably precise about this that it has given rise to many much less precise symbolic interpretations.) To their delight, the disciples found that the net had not been torn.

"Come on, now," coaxed Jesus when the count was over, "and have some breakfast." They complied, all the while casting questioning sidelong glances at him and at one another. They were sure it was Jesus; yet they were not absolutely certain, so they wanted to ask him. But no one was willing to ask what might seem a foolish, perhaps an offensive, question. And so they sat themselves down on the beach amid a general silence and had a hearty breakfast, with Jesus doing the serving.

After breakfast, Jesus and Peter, while the others busied themselves dividing the catch of fish, took a brief walk along the beach. "Peter," asked Jesus, "would you say you love me more than the others?"

"Lord," Peter answered, "you know I love you."

"Then feed my sheep."

They walked on for a moment in silence, Peter not knowing quite how to respond.

"Peter," Jesus asked him again, "do you love me?"

Peter searched Jesus' face for an inkling of what this might be all about. There may have been some crinkling about the eyes, but Peter couldn't be sure. So he played it straight: "Yes, Lord. You know I love you."

"Then take care of my sheep."

Another silence. Then, again he asked, "Peter, do you love me?"

Into Peter's mind crept an embarrassing recollection of his three denials, and sorrow welled up in his heart. "O Lord," he exclaimed, "you know everything, so surely you know I love you."

"Very well," said Jesus for the last time, "take care of my sheep.

"I must tell you something," he continued after a moment's pause. "When you were young, you took care of yourself and went wherever you wanted to go, but when you're old, others will take you in hand and carry you where you don't want to go." This simply puzzled Peter, but John much later, after Peter's death by crucifixion, decided, upon reflection, that Jesus must have had that death in mind.

Yet Peter may have had some suspicion of this, for, according to the record, his next question was about John's ultimate fate. Jesus, however, never much given to casual soothsaying, replied gently that it was none of his business whether or not John would survive until the Second Coming, thereby giving rise to a persistent rumor that John would never die.

Some time thereafter, Jesus again appeared unexpectedly in the midst of the apostles, this time on a mountainside in Galilee. Perhaps as a result of intervening appearances now lost from the record, on this occasion the apostles greeted him with a kind of homage normally reserved for God—though some did so with patent misgivings.

Jesus seems to have responded accordingly, informing them that God had granted him "all authority in heaven and on earth"; they were, therefore, to work for the conversion of all people throughout the world, "baptizing them in the name of the Father and of the Son

and of the Holy Spirit, and teaching them to follow the commandments I've given you. And remember," he added reassuringly, "I'll be
with you always, till the end of time."

His final appearance seems to have been in Jerusalem, from
which he led them out to the Mount of Olives. There he explained—
presumably to help them in their missionary work among the Jews—
how his life, his death at the hands of the authorities, and his
resurrection had fulfilled the scriptural prophecies. In accordance
with the Scriptures, too, they were to carry his message of loving
repentance and forgiveness from Jerusalem out to all humanity. But
first they were to wait in the city until the Father gave them the power
he had promised.

After giving them his blessing, he was lifted toward heaven and
disappeared. When they had shaken off the spell, they returned to
their lodgings in the city. There they stayed for a while, going
frequently to the temple to thank God that Jesus had survived his
final encounter with the authorities. Armed with the knowledge of
that survival and with the help of the Holy Spirit, they would soon
carry abroad his message of divine and human love.

*

Did Jesus really triumph over his adversaries? Even without
accepting his resurrection and other miracles—which, again, are not
impossible, or even improbable as rare occurrences—one must
accept the triumph of the religion that bears his name. Within its first
century, it had grown strong enough to invite official persecution; by
the end of its fourth, it had supplanted the religion of the Roman
Empire; and by its thirteenth, it had become the religion of the
Western World. Today, insofar as the West has a God-centered
religion, that religion is Christianity.

For almost two thousand years, Jesus' message has survived the
toxins introduced by a great variety of authorities: a debilitating
hierarchy and clergy, self-serving councils, contentious sects,
meretricious preachers, paranoid cliques, doctrinaire cynics, evangel-
ical fanatics. Authorities have distorted it with exclusiveness,
superstition, sentimentality, ceremony, institutions, regulations,
regimentation, oppression, torture, fear, pride, and downright
hatred. But through all the establishments and would-be establishments, the message continues to emerge in the direct and simple form
that Jesus gave it: love God and one another, and don't worry about
anything else.

For a poor itinerant preacher whose life ended in execution as a criminal, the mere survival of that message, much less its irrepressible vitality, is surely a glorious victory.

Correlation with Gospel Passages

Prelude

Great Expectations: Matthew 3:1; Mark 1:1; Luke 3:1; John 1:19
Temptation: Matthew 4:1; Mark 1:12; Luke 4:1
The First Disciples: John 1:35
Water into Wine: John 2:1

First Skirmishes: John 2:13

Nicodemus: John 3:1
The Samaritan Woman: John 4:4
"Your Son Will Live": John 4:46
Rejection in Nazareth: Luke 4:16; Matthew 13:54; Mark 6:1 (in this order)
Fishers of Persons: Matthew 4:18; Mark 1:16; Luke 5:1
A Sabbath in Capernaum: Mark 1:21; Luke 4:31
"Your Sins Are Forgiven": Mark 1:35; Luke 4:42; Matthew 9:2 (in this order)
Pious Disapproval: Matthew 9:9; 12:1; Mark 2:13; Luke 5:32; John 5:1

Fall of an Ally: Matthew 12:15; Mark 3:7; Luke 6:12

The Sermon on the Mount: Matthew 5:1; Luke 6:20
The Officer's Servant: Matthew 8:5; Luke 7:1
The Widow's Son: Luke 7:11
The Baptist's Farewell: Matthew 11:2; Luke 7:18
Love and Forgiveness: Luke 7:36

The Devil's Advocates: Matthew 12:22; Mark 3:20; Luke 11:14; 8:19 (in this order)

The Parables: Matthew 13:1; Mark 4:1; Luke 8:4

"Our Name Is Legion": Matthew 8:23; Mark 4:35; Luke 8:22

The Daughter of Jairus: Matthew 9:18; Mark 5:21; Luke 8:40

Advice to the Twelve: Matthew 9:36; Mark 6:7; Luke 9:1

The Death of the Baptist: Matthew 14:1; Mark 6:14; Luke 9:7

Forebodings

The Loaves and Fishes: Matthew 14:13; Mark 6:30; Luke 9:10; John 6:1

Faith on the Surface: Matthew 14:24; Mark 6:47; John 6:16

The Bread of Life: John 6:22

On Cleanliness and Godliness: Matthew 15:1; Mark 7:1

"Who Do You Say I Am?": Matthew 15:21; Mark 7:24

Suffering and Glory: Matthew 16:21; Mark 8:31; Luke 9:22

Threat and Defiance: Matthew 17:24

On Humility and Forgiveness: Matthew 18:1; Mark 9:33; Luke 9:46

A Source of Dissension: John 7:1

"I Am": John 8:1

Samaritans, Unfriendly and Otherwise: Matthew 8:18; Mark 10:1; Luke 9:51

The Divine Shepherd: Luke 10:38; John 9:1

"I and the Father": John 10:22

The Menacing Fox: Luke 13:1

To the Lions' Den: Luke 14:1

The Prodigal Son: Luke 15:1

The Perils of Wealth: Luke 16:1

Resurrection and Alarm: John 11:1

The Second Coming: Luke 17:11

On Pride in Hearts and Husbands: Luke 18:9; Matthew 19:3; Mark 10:2 (in this order)

The Rewards of Detachment: Matthew 19:16; Mark 10:17; Luke 18:18

A Role for Authority: Matthew 20:17; Mark 10:32; Luke 18:31

A Stopover in Jericho: Matthew 20:29; Mark 10:46; Luke 18:35

A Farewell Party: Matthew 26:6; Mark 14:3; John 11:55

Defeat: Matthew 21:1; Mark 11:1; Luke 19:29; John 12:12

Trouble in the Temple: Matthew 21:12; Mark 11:15; Luke 19:45

In No Uncertain Terms: Matthew 22:15; Mark 12:13; Luke 20:20

Intimations of the Cross: John 12:20

An Apocalyptic Interlude: Matthew 24:1; Mark 13:1; Luke 21:5

The Last Supper: Matthew 26:1; Mark 14:1; Luke 22:1; John 13:1

A Farewell Address: John 13:31

Gethsemane: Matthew 26:36; Mark 14:32; Luke 22:39; John 18:1

Trial by Ordeal: Matthew 26:57; Mark 14:53; Luke 22:54; John 18:12

The Long Arm of Rome: Matthew 27:2; Mark 15:1; Luke 23:1; John 18:28

The Cross: Matthew 27:32; Mark 15:21; Luke 23:26; John 19:16

The Tomb: John 19:31; Matthew 27:57; Mark 15:42; Luke 23:50 (in this order)

Victory: Matthew 28:1; Mark 16:1; Luke 23:56; John 20:1

Keeping Up Appearances: Mark 16:12; Luke 24:13; John 20:19; Matthew 28:16 (in this order)

The Bible passages are identified by the first verse.

Sources

Primary Sources

Buttrick, George Arthur, *et al., The Interpreter's Bible.* Nashville: Abingdon-Cokesbury Press, 1951.

Good News Bible. New York: American Bible Society, 1976.

The Gospels. Trans. J. B. Phillips. New York: Macmillan, Inc., 1953.

Grispino, Joseph A., *The New Testament of the Holy Bible* (Confraternity Version). New York: Guild Press, 1966.

The Holy Bible (Douay-Rheims Version). Baltimore: John Murphy Co., 1914.

Kleist, James A., and Lilly, Joseph L., eds., *The New Testament.* Encino, Calif.: Bruce Publishing Co., 1956.

Stevens, William Arnold, and Burton, Ernest DeWitt, *A Harmony of the Gospels for Historical Study.* New York: Charles Scribner's Sons, 1904.

Related Reading

Anderson, Hugh, ed., *Jesus.* Englewood Cliffs, N.J.: Prentice-Hall, Inc., 1967.

Austin, Mary H., *The Man Jesus.* New York: Harper & Row, Publishers, Inc., 1915.

Barbet, Pierre, *A Doctor at Calvary.* New York: P. J. Kenedy & Sons, 1954.

Barton, Bruce, *The Man Nobody Knows.* Indianapolis: Bobbs-Merrill Co., Inc., 1925.

Buck, Pearl S., *The Story Bible: The New Testament,* vol. 2. New York: New American Library, Inc., 1972.

Carmichael, Joel, *The Death of Jesus.* New York: Macmillan, Inc., 1962.

Case, Shirley Jackson, *Jesus.* Chicago: University of Chicago Press, 1927.

Chute, Marchette, *Jesus of Israel.* New York: E. P. Dutton and Elsevier Book Operations, 1961.

Daniel-Rops, Henry, *Jesus and His Times.* New York: E. P. Dutton and Elsevier Book Operations, 1956.

Deane, Anthony C., *The World Christ Knew.* East Lansing, Mich.: Michigan State University Press, 1953.

Erskine, John, *The Human Life of Jesus.* New York: Garden City Books, 1949.

Fouard, Constant, *The Life of Christ.* New York: Guild Press, 1954.

Glover, T. R., *Jesus in the Experience of Men.* Wilton, Conn.: Association Press, 1921.

_____, *The Jesus of History.* London: SCM Press, 1917.

Goodspeed, Edgar J., *A Life of Jesus.* New York: Harper & Row, Publishers, Inc., 1950.

Grant, Michael, *Jesus: An Historian's Review of the Gospels.* New York: Charles Scribner's Sons, 1977.

The Holy Bible. Trans. Ronald Knox. Mission, Kans.: Sheed Andrews & McMeel, Inc., 1956.

Kung, Hans, *On Being a Christian.* New York: Doubleday & Co., Inc., 1976.

Lamsa, George M., *More Light on the Gospel.* New York: Doubleday & Co., Inc., 1968.

Ludwig, Emil, *The Son of Man.* New York: Liveright, subsidiary of W. W. Norton & Co., Inc., 1928.

Muggeridge, Malcolm, *Jesus: The Man Who Lives.* New York: Harper & Row, Publishers, Inc., 1975.

Oursler, Fulton, *The Greatest Story Ever Told.* New York: Doubleday & Co., Inc., 1949.

Papini, Giovanni, *Life of Christ.* New York: Harcourt Brace Jovanovich, 1923.

Paul, Leslie, *Son of Man: The Life of Christ.* New York: E. P. Dutton and Elsevier Book Operations, 1961.

Phipps, William E., *Recovering Biblical Sensuousness.* Philadelphia: The Westminster Press, 1975.

Renan, Ernest, *The Life of Jesus.* Derby, Conn.: Belmont-Tower Books, 1972.

Schonfield, Hugh J., *The Passover Plot.* London: Hutchinson & Co., 1965.

Schweitzer, Albert, *The Quest of the Historical Jesus.* New York: Macmillan, Inc., 1961.

Sheen, Fulton J., *Life of Christ.* New York: McGraw-Hill Book Co., 1958.

Stauffer, Ethelbert, *Jesus and His Story.* New York: Alfred A. Knopf, Inc., 1960.

Trueblood, David Elton, *The Humor of Christ.* New York: Harper & Row, Publishers, Inc., 1964.

Vigeveno, H. S., *Jesus the Revolutionary.* Glendale, Calif.: Gospel Light Press, 1966.

Index

Abraham, 11, 12, 71, 72, 73, 80, 84, 85,
  94
Andrew, 14, 25, 104
Annas, 115, 116
Authorities, 11, 12, 18, 19, 27, 28, 29,
  30, 31, 32, 33, 39, 40, 43, 54, 58, 62,
  67, 68, 69, 70, 71, 76, 77, 78, 79, 80,
  84, 87, 88, 90, 96, 97, 100, 102, 103,
  105, 107, 116, 117, 118, 121

Barabbas, 119
Bethany, 73, 75, 85, 86, 93, 95
Bethesda, 29
Bethsaida, 14, 61, 104
"Born again," 19

Caesar, 100, 118
Caiaphas, 87, 115, 116
Cana, 14, 23
Capernaum, 17, 23, 24, 25, 27, 38, 47,
  54, 55, 65
Cleophas, 127
Corban, 58

Divorce, 90

Elijah, 24, 62, 63, 64
Emmaus, 126, 127
Ephraim, 87

Fasting, 13, 29

Galilee, Galileans, 12, 14, 20, 22, 26, 60,
  64, 67, 69, 73, 79, 80
Gethsemane, 114
Golgotha, 120

Herod Antipas, 19, 20, 50, 53, 80, 119

Isaiah, 11, 58

Jairus, 47
James, 25, 35, 63, 93, 114
Jericho, 93, 94
Jerusalem, 11, 12, 17, 21, 22, 29, 58, 62,
  67, 73, 78, 80, 81, 92, 97, 98, 104,
  126, 127
Jesus Christ
  associations, 28, 29, 41, 42, 43, 83
  baptism, 12, 13
  bread of life, 57
  death, 64, 93, 105, 120-122
  family, 67
  miracles, 14, 15, 18, 23, 25, 26, 27, 28,
    30, 33, 39, 40, 46, 47, 48, 54, 55,
    59, 60, 64, 75, 80, 87, 94, 115,
    125, 126
  temptation, 13
  transfiguration, 63
John the Apostle, 25, 35, 63, 67, 93, 114,
  122, 125, 129, 130
John the Baptist, 11, 12, 13, 19, 20, 29,
  31, 40, 50, 51, 62, 64, 79, 99

Joseph, 14, 24, 56
Joseph of Arimathea, 123
Judas, 35, 96, 107, 108, 109, 115, 117
Judea, 11, 12, 67, 73, 79, 85

Lazarus, 85-87, 95, 96, 97
Lord's Prayer, 37

Martha, 75, 85, 86, 95
Mary (Jesus' mother), 15, 44, 56, 122
Mary Magdalene, 42, 122, 123, 125, 126
Mary of Bethany, 75, 85, 86, 95, 96
Messiah, 11, 12, 14, 17, 18, 22, 62, 63,
    69, 78, 97, 103, 127
Moses, 63, 68, 90, 102
Mount Gerizim, 20, 21
Mount Hermon, 61, 63
Mount of Olives, 98, 109, 114

Nain, 39
Nathanael, 14
Nazareth, 14, 23, 24, 25, 69
Nicodemus, 18, 19, 20, 69, 123

Parables, 44, 45, 66, 67, 79, 82-85, 89,
    90, 92, 94, 95, 99
Passover, 17, 22, 81, 104, 107
Perea, 20, 73

Peter, 14, 24, 25, 26, 35, 55, 58, 59, 62,
    63, 65, 91, 108, 109, 114, 115, 117,
    125, 127, 129, 130
Pharisees (see authorities), 18
Philip, 14, 104, 110
Pilate, 79, 117, 118, 119, 120, 123
Prodigal son, 82

Sabbath, 11, 25, 26, 30, 32, 33, 68, 80
Sadducees (see authorities), 18
Samaria, Samaritans, 12, 19, 20, 22, 56,
    73, 74, 88
Sea of Galilee (Lake Gennesaret), 14,
    17, 24
Sermon on the Mount, 35-38
Simon (see Peter)
Simon the Leper, 95
Spirit of truth, 112
Sychar, 20

Tax collectors, 28, 29, 65, 94, 99
Temple (Jerusalem), 17, 18, 20, 30, 32,
    78, 98, 106
Thomas, 86, 110, 128

Widow's mite, 104

Zacchaeus, 94

BT   25314
301.2
B181   Baldwin
1979   Jesus of Galilee

BT   25314
301.2
B181   Baldwin
1979   Jesus of Galilee